The Insurance Market in Latin America, Portugal, and Spain

The Insurance Market in Latin America, Portugal, and Spain

JULIO CASTELO
Director of the Study

Assisted by

EMILIO CORONADO
LUIS HERNANDO DE LARRAMENDI
JOSÉ MA. FERNÁNDEZ PASTRANA
GERARDO MENÉNDEZ ARRÚE
MARK R. GREENE

UNIVERSITY OF GEORGIA PRESS

Athens

Contents

Foreword

INSURANCE is basically an institutional activity, and more than any other economic service, it requires international coordination. Thus, the assembled information coming from different markets with similar characteristics becomes an important means of improvement and creates new links of union and reciprocal influence among countries. Both the key Latin American markets and those of the Iberian Penninsula share not only two mutually corresponding languages, but also many similar economic and sociological features.

Mapfre Insurance Group and its subsidiary company, Mapfre Estudios, felt that they could offer to the Spanish- and Portuguese-speaking countries an important institutional study which will contribute in some way to strengthen the links of brotherhood and provide them with a structural and comprehensive analysis of insurance activity. This first volume explains the legal and institutional aspects, and the second volume the economic and financial issues.

Since 1969, when I first attended a Hemispheric Insurance Congress, I have been encouraging this project; and now, as general director of the Mapfre Group, I want to express my full confidence in the future of the countries mentioned in this book and my deep hope that the effort made by Mapfre and everyone cooperating in this work may constitute a useful contribution to the coordinated development of Iberian and Latin American insurance activity.

Ignacio H. de Larramendi

Introduction

THIS work is an analysis of the key features that characterize the insurance markets of the major Latin American countries from several points of view: legal, technical, operative, economic, and statistical.

The preparation of this book was laborious and complex because of the singular nature of the subjects included. It was based on a series of assumptions that require some explanation, thus permitting the reader to obtain an insight into the general lines of methodology used and the limits accepted. Among the many technical studies consulted in this comparative analysis of insurance markets, we must mention specially *Control of Private Insurance in Europe,*[1] *World Insurance Markets,*[2] and *Studies on the Insurance Government Control,* a legal comparison between Europe and Iberoamerica.[3] Although the orientation and extent of this study is different, these books have been an excellent source for consultation.

The geographical scope of this book is limited to South America, Mexico, Portugal, and Spain. Our first idea was to include the Central American countries, but because of the limitation of our own means of research and the context of this book, we felt that the inclusion of those countries would have postponed excessively the publication of the information. Many concepts or figures which refer to the other countries would then have become obsolete.

The context of this book differs from comparatively similar studies. Its two parts show the parallel between what is institutional and what is statistical-economic in each market and on the entities involved. We have omitted personal comment about legal rules, factual situations, or resulting figures. Although important conclusions might come from our commentaries, this operation is left to the reader's imagination.

The institutional portion of this volume is classified under the following headings: (1) General Information, (2) Form and Operation of Private Insurers, (3) Contracting, (4) Technical Reserves, (5) Reinsurance, (6) Taxes, (7) Production (Agents), (8) Institutional Bodies, (9) Characteristics of the Sixties, and (10) Fundamental Legislation.

These headings are used in the study of each of the thirteen countries

---

1. M. Paratte (Switzerland), Director of the Study Group. Economic Organization for Cooperation and Development (EOCD). Edited in Paris, 1963.

2. Dr. Max E. Eisrling, Director of the Study. Edited in Zurich, 1964, by the Swiss Reinsurance Company (centenary edition).

3. D. Ernesto Caballero Sanchez, Edited in Madrid, 1966, by the Centro de Investigaciones y Estudios del Seguro Iberoamericano (CIESI)—Research and Studies Center of the Iber American Insurance Co.

included in this study. This feature of our work gives a more accurate, brief, and flexible reading of the text by means of a summarized sketch and homogenous information which makes it easier to understand the comparison among countries. This method, however, forces us to organize the material in preestablished schemes, and the various peculiarities of every country may be rather faintly portrayed.

Two appendixes appear at the end of this volume; one containing a series of inferences drawn from an overall analysis of the countries in view and the other introducing the report concerning the legal insurance statutes and supervision in developing countries. This latter was prepared by a group of experts in 1971 on the request of the United National Conference for Trade and Development (UNCTAD).

The authors feel that important conclusions will come from the comparative information among countries included in the statistical and economic portion of the second volume of this book. In each case we find three levels of information: those from macro-economic sources, from key private entities, and from the insuring market itself. The diagrams and charts will be conceived in the framework of the comparative principles accepted among insurance activities.

Finally we wish to express our gratitude to the following persons and institutions which have contributed to the preparation of this work by providing information, reviewing, supervision, and suggestions, with the hope that they will continue to contribute for the second volume on economic and statistical issues:

In Argentina, Amigo, Valenti y Cía, Contadores Auditores, Buenos Aires; Jorge Marcelo Benchetrit, manager of Centro de Estudios e Investigaciones del Seguro, Buenos Aires; Juan Carlos Félix Morandi, professor of Commercial Law at the Universidad Santa María de los Buenos Aires, Buenos Aires; Guillermo Moreno Hueyo, president of La Franco Argentina, C. A., Buenos Aires; Alberto C. Passaró, insurance manager of Caja Nacional de Ahorro Postal, Buenos Aires; Carlos A. Pollitzer, managing director of Pollitzer, S. A., Buenos Aires; Ruben S. Stiglitz, editor of Revista de Derecho de Seguros, La Plata.

In Bolivia, C. Adams Elío M., manager of Compañía Boliviana de Seguros, S. A., La Paz; Guillermo Fernández G., general manager of La Oriental de Seguros, La Paz; Antonio Hernández M, general manager of La Mercantil de Seguros y Reaseguros, S. A., La Paz.

In Brazil, Joao Carlos de Almeida Braga, manager of Grupo Atlántica-Boavista de Seguros, Río de Janeiro; Oswaldo de Castro Santos, manager of Companhia Seguradora Brasileira, São Paulo; Angelo Mario Cerne, vice-president of Companhia Internacional de Seguros, Río de Janeiro; Weber José Ferreira, manager Instituto de Resseguros do Brasil (I.R.B.), Río de Janeiro; José Lopes de Oliveira, president of Instituto de Resseguros do Brasil (I.R.B.), Río de Janeiro; Antonio C. Pacheco e Silva, president of Grupo Segurador

Brasil, São Paulo; Edilmar Passos, manager of the technical department of Superintendencia de Seguros Privados, Río de Janeiro; Raul Telles Rudge, manager of La Sul-América, Río de Janeiro.

In Colombia, Luis Armenta Daza, superintendent of insurance, Bogotá; Guillermo Baca Currea, manager of Compañía Colombiana de Seguros, Bototá; Jaime Bustamente Ferrer, president of Asociación Colombiana de Compañías de Seguros, Bogotá; Saúl Flórez, manager of the Legal Department, Compañía de Seguros Bolívar, Bogotá; Luciano Herrera R, vice-president of Compañía Colombiana de Seguros, Bogotá; Hernán F. López Blanco, manager of the Legal Department, Compañía de Seguros Bolívar, Bogotá; J. Efrén Ossa G., president of Asociación Colombiana de Derecho de Seguros, Bototá; Rodrigo Vázquez, general manager of Reaseguradora de Colombia, Bogotá; Gustavo Vega B., vice-president of Suramericana de Seguros, Medellín.

In Chile, Jorge Bande, president of La Chilena Consolidada, Santiago de Chile; Rusell Beckett Lackington, manager of Insurance Department of Compañías de Seguros de la Superintendencia de Seguros, Santiago de Chile; Hernán Errázuriz Talavera, lawyer, Santiago de Chile; D. René Labbé, manager of La Chilena Consolidada, Santiago de Chile; Luis Soffia, general manager of Consorcio Nacional de Seguros, Santiago de Chile; Francisco Tagle, manager of Consorcio Nacional de Seguros, Santiago de Chile; Hernán Valdivieso Echevarría, manager of Consorcio Nacional de Seguros, Santiago de Chile; Raúl Venegas Marín, manager of Caja Reaseguradora de Chile, Santiago de Chile.

In Ecuador, Dagoberto Saltos Paredes, insurance manager of the Superintendencia de Bancos y Seguros, Quito.

In Mexico, Mariano de Cárcer, manager of Seguros América Banamex, S. A., México, D. F.; George Holden, general manager of Monterrey, Compañía de Seguros, S. A., México, D. F.; Emilio Portes Gil, president of Comisión Nacional de Seguros, México, D. F.; Werner A. Roth, manager of Seguros de México Bancomer, S. A., México, D. F.; Francisco Ureña Corta, general manager of Reaseguradora Patria, S. A., México, D. F.; Mario Zerecero Acosta, manager of Seguros de Mexico Bancomer, S. A., México, D. F.

In Paraguay, Ricardo Justino Arce, manager of Division Contralor de Seguros del Banco Central del Paraguay, Asunción; César Avalos, general manager of Segesa, Seguros Generales, S. A., Asunción; Víctor José Beckelmann, Superintendent of Banks, Asunción; Pastor C. Filártiga, manager of Asociación Paraguaya de Compañías de Seguros, Asunción; Juan Carlos Martincich, manager of Planeta, S. A., Seguros y Reaseguros, Asunción.

In Peru, Juan Francisco Ropero Plá, manager of El Pacífico, S. A., Lima; Amadeo Vallejo Lasanta, manager of El Pacífico, S. A., Lima.

In Portugal, José de Castro Sales Herinques, Inspección General de Crédito y Seguros, Lisboa; Manuel S. Soares Povoas, general manager of Mutualidade, Lisboa.

In Spain, Ernesto Caballero Sánchez, managing director of Mutualidad de

Seguros del I.N.I. (MUSINI), Madrid; Foreign Department of Banco Español de Crédito, Madrid.

In Uruguay, Héctor Cerruti Aicardi, president of Sección Paraguaya de la Asociación Internacional de Derecho de Seguros, Montevideo; Antonio H. Picón, manager of Dpto. de Inversiones, Organización y Método del Banco de Seguros del Estado, Montevideo.

In Venezuela, Pedro de Aguirrezábal, manager of C. A. La Seguridad, Caracas; Konrad Firgau Yanes, manager of Escuela Superior de Seguros, Caracas; Godofredo Martínez Linares, manager of Horizonte, C. A. de Seguros, Caracas; Fernando Varela Llanos, manager of Riesgos Especiales de Seguros Caracas, Caracas; Eduardo Wallis Olavarria, superintendent of Insurance, Ministerio de Fomento, Caracas.

Insurance Organizations

ARGENTINA

Argentinian Actuaries Institute	Instituto Argentino de Actuarios
Argentinian Association of Insurance Companies	Asociación Argentina de Compañías de Seguros
Argentinian Foreign Insurers Association	Asociación de Aseguradores Extranjeros en la Argentina
Argentinian Insurers Committee	Comité de Aseguradores Argentinos
Argentinian National Bank	Banco de la Nación Argentina
Foreign Insurers Association	Asociación de Aseguradores Extranjeros
General Inspection of Juristic Entities	Inspección General de Personas Jurídicas
Hemispheric Insurance Conference	Conferencia Hemisférica de Seguros
Insurance Assessors Producers Association	Asociación de Productores Asesores de Seguros
Insurance Autonomous Institute of Entre Ríos	Instituto Autárquico del Seguro de Entre Ríos
Insurance Companies Association	Asociación de Compañías Aseguradoras
Insurers Chamber	Cámara de Aseguardores
Insurance Chamber of the Argentinian Republic	Cámara de Aseguardores de la República Argentina
Insurance Professional School	Escuela Profesional del Seguro
Insurance Studies and Research Center	Centro de Estudios e Investigación del Seguro
Insurance Workers Trade Union	Sindicato del Seguro
Mutual and Cooperative Association	Asociación de Cooperativas y Mutualidades
Ministry of Labor	Ministerio del Trabajo
Ministry of Social Welfare	Ministerio de Bienestar Social
Ministry of Treasure and Finance	Ministerio de Hacienda y Finanzas
Mutual and Cooperative Consultative Committee	Comisión Consultiva de Cooperativas y Mutualidades
National Dept. of Cooperatives	Departamento Nacional de Cooperativas
National Executive Power	Poder Ejecutivo Nacional
National Institute for Social Provision	Instituto Nacional de Previsión Social
National Insurance Supervisory Office	Superintendencia de Seguros de la Nación
National Postal Saving Bank	Caja Nacional de Ahorro Postal
National Reinsurance Institute	Instituto Nacional de Reaseguros
Official Bulletin	Boletín Oficial
Popular Saving Bank	Caja Popular de Ahorro
Provincial Insurance Institute	Instituto Provincial del Seguro
Register of Insurance Entities	Registro de Entidades de Seguros
Retirement Bank	Caja de Jubilaciones
Syndical Chamber of Insurers	Cámara Sindical de Aseguradores

BOLIVIA

Banks Supervisory Office	Superintendencia de Bancos
Bolivian Insurers Association	Asociación Boliviana de Aseguradores
Compulsory Social Security	Seguro Social Obligatorio
Confederation of Private Entrepreneurs of Bolivia	Confederación de Empresarios Privados de Bolivia
Fiscalization Division of the Bank Supervisory Office	División de Fiscalización de la Superintendencia de Bancos
Housing Saving and Loans Central Fund	Caja Central de Ahorro y Préstamos para la Vivienda
Insurance and Capitalization Register	Departamento de Seguro de la Superintendencia de Bancos
Insurance Department of the Bank Supervisory Office	Registro de Seguro y Capitalización
Loss Liquidators Division	Departamento de Liquidación de Siniestros
National Compulsory Social Security Fund	Caja Nacional de Seguro Social Obligatorio
National Chamber of Commerce	Cámara Nacional de Comercio

BRAZIL

Reinsurance Institute of Brazil	Instituto de Resseguros do Brasil (IRB)
Ministry of Trade and Industry	Ministério da Industria e do Comércio
Private Insurance National Council	Conselho Nacional de Seguros Privados (CNSP)
Private Insurance Supervisory Office	Superintendência de Seguros Privados (SUSEP)
National Federation of Private Insurance Companies and Capitalization	Federação Nacional das Empresas de Seguros Privados e de Capitalização (FENASEG)
Insurance General Supervisory Office	Superintendência Geral de Seguros
Ministry of the Treasure	Ministerio de Fazenda
Social Security National Institute	Instituto Nacional de Previdência Social
Central Bank of Brazil	Banco Central do Brasil
National Monetary Council	Conselho Monétario Nacional (CMN)
Official Journal of the Union	"Diário Oficial" da União
Foreign Trade National Council	Conselho Nacional de Comércio Exterior
Brazilian Insurance Science Society	Sociedade Brasileira de Ciências do Seguro
Insurance National School	Escola Nacional de Seguros
Brazilian Actuaries Institute	Instituto Brasileiro de Atuária
International Insurance Laws Association	Asociação International de Dereito No Seguros
Brokers Union Register	Registro Sindical de Corretores
National Bank for Economic Development	Banco Nacional de Desenvolvimento
Inland Insurers Federation	Federação de Seguradores Terrestres
Insurance Brokers Regional Trade Unions	Sindicatos Regionais de Corretores de Seguros
Insurance Companies National Trade Unions	Sindicatos Nacionais de Sociedades Seguradoras

Ministry of General Planning and Coordination — Ministerio de Planificação e Coordinação

CHILE

Association of Claims Adjusters — Asociación de Liquidadores de Averías
Association of Insurers of Chile — Asociación de Aseguradores de Chile
Bank of the Government of Chile — Banco del Estado de Chile
Educational Institutes Building Society — Sociedad Constructora de Establecimientos Educacionales
Insurance Companies, Stock Associations and Stock Exchange Supervisory Office — Superintendencia de Compañías de Seguros Sociedades Anónimas y Bolsas de Comercio
Insurance Producers National Union — Sindicato Nacional de Productores de Seguros
Life Insurance Association — Asociación de Aseguradores sobre la Vida
National Company of Export Credit Insurance — Compañía Nacional de Seguro de Crédito a la Exportación
National Health Service — Servicio Nacional de Salud
Provision Funds — Cajas de Previsión
Reinsurance Fund of Chile — Caja Reaseguradora de Chile
Reinsurance Syndicate — Unión de Reaseguros
Social Insurance Service — Servicio de Seguro Social

COLUMBIA

Agrarian, Industrial and Mining Loan Fund — Caja de Crédito Agrario, Industrial y Minero
Bank of the Republic — Banco de la República
Banking Superintendancy Register — Registro de la Superintendencia Bancaria
Bank Supervisory Office — Superintendencia Bancaria
Colombian Association of Insurance Agents — Asociación Colombiana de Agentes de Seguros (ACODASE)
Colombian Association of Insurance Brokers — Asociación Colombiana de Corredores de Seguros
Colombian Association of Insurance Companies — Asociación Colombiana de Compañías de Seguros (ASECOLDA)
Colombian Association of Insurance Law — Asociación Colombiana de Derecho de Seguros
Colombian Social Insurance Institute — Instituto Colombiano de Seguros Sociales
Colombian Reinsurance Company — Compañía Reaseguradora de Colombia
Commerce Public Register — Registro Público de Comercio
Cooperative National Supervisory Office — Superintendencia Nacional de Cooperativas
Consulting Council of Actuaries — Consejo Consultivo de Actuarios
Consulting Commission of Insurance — Comisión Consultiva de Seguros
Economic Law and Sciences Faculties — Facultades de Derecho y Ciencias Económicas

Insurance Faculty	Facultad de Seguro
Insurance Studies Center	Centro de Estudios del Seguro
Lawyers Insurance Companies	Compañías de Seguros de Juristas
Mortgage Central Bank	Banco Central Hipotecario
Professional Insurance and Reinsurance College	Escuela Profesional de Seguros y Reaseguro
Professional Unions of Insurance Producers	Sindicatos Profesionales de Productores de Seguros
Provisional National Fund	Caja Nacional de Previsión
Stock Company Superintendency	Superintendencia de Sociedades Anónimas
Security Inscription Board	Junta de Inscripción de Títulos
Territorial Credit Institute	Instituto de Crédito Territorial

ECUADOR

Agents Unions	Sindicato de Agentes
Association of Insurance Companies in Ecuador	Asociación de Compañías de Seguros en el Ecuador
Banks Superintendency	Superintendencia de Bancos
Brokers Agents Union	Sindicato de Agentes Corredores
Chamber of Insurance Companies in Ecuador	Cámara de Compañías de Seguros en Ecuador
Commerce Register	Registro Mercantil
Fomenting Credit System Banks	Bancos de Sistema de Crédito de Fomento
Ecuadorian Fire Insurance Company	Compañía Ecuatoriana de Seguros contra Incendios
Ecuadorian Housing Bank	Banco Ecuatoriano de la Vivienda
Ecuadorian Social Insurance	Seguro Social Ecuatoriano
Employment Agencies	Agencias Colocadoras
Guayaquil National Insurance Company	Compañía Nacional de Seguros de Guayaquil
Monetary Board	Junta Monetaria
Mortgage Bank	Banco Hipotecario
Mortgage Sections of Commercial Bank	Secciones Hipotecarias de los Bancos Comerciales
National Financial Corporation	Corporación Financiera Nacional
Official Register	Registro Oficial
Official Reinsurance Committee	Comité Oficial de Reaseguros
Supreme Court of Justice	Corte Suprema de Justicia
Values Commission	Comisión de Valores

MEXICO

Alianza Reinsurance Corporation	Sociedad Anónima de Reaseguro Alianza
Insurance Division of the Secretary of Treasury	Departamento de Seguros del Ministerio de Hacienda

Mexican Association of Fire Insurance Agency	Asociación Mexicana de Agentes de Seguros de Incendio
Mexican Association of Technical Insurance and Surety Agency	Asociación Mexicana de Agentes Técnicos de Seguro y Fianzas
Mexican Institute of Social Security	Instituto Mexicano de Seguridad Social
National Banking Commission of Insurance and Sureties	Comisión Nacional Bancaria y de Seguros y Finanzas
National Commission of Values	Comisión Nacional de Valores
National Insurance Commission	Comisión Nacional de Seguro
"Patria" Reinsurance Corporation	Sociedad Anónima de Reaseguros "Patria"
Public Register of Commerce	Registro Público de Comercio
Secretary of the Treasury and Public Credit	Secretaría de Hacienda y Crédito Público

PARAGUAY

Bank Supervisory Office	Superintendencia de Bancos
Central Railway of Paraguay	Ferrocarril Central de Paraguay
Chamber of Motorvehicles Insurers	Cámara de Aseguradores de Automotores
Directorate of the Central Bank of Paraguay	Directorio del Banco Central de Paraguay
Insurance Companies Associations	Asociación de Compañías de Seguros
Insurance Supervisory Office	Superintendencia de Seguros
Insurers Association	Gremio de Aseguradores
Latin American Reinsurance Pool	Pool Latinoamericano de Reaseguros

PERU

Bank and Insurance Supervisory Office	Superintendencia de Banca y Seguro
Credit Insurance Company	Compañía de Seguro de Crédito
Deposits and Consignations Fund	Caja de Depósitos y Consignaciones
Fiscal Inspection	Inspección Fiscal
Insurance Training School	Escuela de Capacitación de Seguros
Ministry of Treasury and Commerce	Ministerio de Hacienda y Comercio
National Bank	Banco de la Nación
Peruvian Insurers Association	Asociación de Aseguradores de Perú
Public Register	Registro Público

PORTUGAL

Credit and Insurance Company	Compañía de Crédito y Seguro
Credit and Insurance General Inspection	Inspección General de Crédito y Seguro
Employees Trade Union	Sindicato de Empleados
General Company of Portuguese Predial Credit	Compañía General de Crédito Predial Portuguesa

Insurance Credit Corporation	Sociedad Anónima de Crédito de Seguros
Insurance Inspection	Inspección de Seguros
Insurers Association	Gremio de Aseguradores
Ministry of Finance	Ministerio de Hacienda
Municipal Chambers	Cámaras Municipales
National Insurance Board	Consejo Nacional de Seguros
National Syndicate of Insurance Professionals	Sindicato Nacional de Profesionales del Seguro
Portuguese Actuaries Institute	Instituto de Actuarios Portugueses
Portuguese Branch of the International Association of Insurance Law	Sección Portuguesa de la Asociación Internacional de Derecho de Seguro
Portuguese Merchants Society	Sociedad de Mercaderes Portugueses
Register of Insurance Companies	Registro de Compañías de Seguros

SPAIN

Accident Prevention Association	Asociación para la Prevención de Accidentes
Actuaries Spanish Institute	Instituto Español de Actuarios
Aviation Risks Insurance Group	Agrupación de Aseguradores de Riesgos de Aviación (AGARA)
Bank of Spain	Banco de España
Center of Iberamerican Insurance Studies and Research	Centro de Estudios e Investigación del Seguro Iberoamericano (CIESI)
Cooperative Research Among Ensuring Entities	Investigación Cooperativa entre Entidades Aseguradoras (ICEA)
Direct Taxes General Direction	Dirección General de Impuestos Directos
Employers Mutual	Mutuas Patronales
General Subdirection of Insurances	Subdirección General de Seguros
Insurance Arbitration Court	Tribunal Arbitral de Seguros
Insurance Compensation Consortium	Consorcio de Compensación de Seguros
Insurance Consulting Board	Junta Consultiva de Seguros
Labor Mutuals	Mutualidades Laborales
Ministry of Work	Ministerio del Trabajo
National Association of Agents	Colegio Nacional de Agentes
National Fund of Traffic Risks Guaranty	Fondo Nacional de Garantía de Riesgos de la Circulación
National Industry Institute Mutual Insurance Association	Mutualidad de Seguros del INI (MUSINI)
National Insurance Union	Sindicato Nacional del Seguro
National Unions	Uniones Nacionales
Spanish Association of Claims Liquidators	Asociación Española de Liquidadores de Averías
Spanish Automobile Insurance Office	Oficina Española de Aseguradores de Automóviles (OFESAUTO)

Spanish Company for Export Credit Insurance	Sociedad Española de Seguro de Crédito a la Exportación
Spanish Company of Credit and Bail	Compañía Española de Crédito y Caución
Spanish Institute of Foreign Currency	Instituto Español de Moneda Extranjera
Spanish Maritime Commissariat	Comisariado Español Marítimo
Spanish Section of the International Association of Insurance Law	Sección Española de la Asociación Internacional de Derecho de Seguros
Spanish Tourist Insurance Group	Agrupación para el Seguro Turístico Español
Technical Corps of Inspectors of Insurance and Savings	Cuerpo Técnico de Inspectores de Seguro y Ahorros
Union Service for Automobile Special Risks	Servicio Sindical de Riesgos Especiales de Automóviles

URUGUAY

Central Bank of Uruguay	Banco Central de Uruguay
Finance and Stock Companies General Inspection	Inspección General de Hacienda y Sociedades Anónimas
Fire Underwriters Committees	Comité de Aseguradores contra Incendio
International Association of Insurance Law	Asociación Internacional de Derecho de Seguros
Local Committee of Fire Insurance Underwriters	Comité Local de Aseguradores Contra Incendios
Permanent Committees of the Underwriters Association	Comités Permanentes de la Asociación de Aseguradores
Senate	Cámara de Senadores
Social Security Bank	Banco de Previsión Social
State Insurance Bank	Banco de Seguros del Estado

VENEZUELA

Fiscal Authority of Insurance Enterprises	Fiscalía de Empresas de Seguros
Insurance Supervisory Office	Superintendencia de Seguro
Ministry of Development	Ministerio de Fomento
National Insurance Board	Consejo Nacional de Seguros
Venezuelan Chamber of Insurance Brokerage Companies	Cámara Venezolana de Sociedades de Corretaje de Seguros
Venezuelan College of Insurance Agents and Brokers	Colegio Venezolano de Agentes y Corredores de Seguros
Venezuelan Institute of Social Insurance	Instituto Venezolano de Seguro Social

Argentina

I. GENERAL INFORMATION

Historical Note. The first insurance company to begin operations in Argentina was the Royal Terrestrial and Marine Insurance Co. of Madrid in 1784.

The first native Argentinian company was La Confianza, established in 1796 for a five-year term. During this time it provided normal insurance services. Three foreign insurance companies—the Northern Assurance Co., Royal Insurance Co. and La Española—were established in 1856. The first Argentinian marine insurance company, founded in 1860, operated for eighteen years.

The Argentinian Insurers Committee, a forerunner of the syndical Chamber of Insurers, was instituted at the end of the nineteenth century. La Rural, an Argentinian company, began to cover hailstorm damage about this time.

The Argentinian government began to regulate insurance activities during the first third of the twentieth century, and in 1938 the Insurance Supervisory Office was established.

Official Control. This Insurance Supervisory Office was a branch of the Ministry of the Treasury and Finance, and it regulates government activities in the supervision of insurance. The National Reinsurance Institute also regulates insurance activities.

Professional Organizations. The three major organizations for insurers are the Argentinian Association of Insurance Companies, the Foreign Insurers Association, and the Mutual and Cooperative Societies Association. Individual agents may belong to the Insurance Agents and Producers Association. Other employees may join the Insurance Workers Trade Union.

These organizations have a brotherhood or guild-like character, supporting their members' professional interests.

Market Structure. The market is composed of 290 groups, including 180 stock companies, 61 cooperatives, 5 mutual societies, 36 branch offices of foreign companies, and 8 government bodies.

The distribution of premiums among these groups includes stock companies, fifty-seven, 16%; mutual and cooperative societies, twenty, 75%; foreign companies, four, 33%; and government organizations, seventeen, 76%.

Automobile and life insurance are the most important lines, representing 55 and 15% respectively in the total market.

International Expansion. International expansion has been limited with only a few Argentinian companies establishing branch offices in foreign companies; even these operations are marginal.

Workmen's Compensation. Although workmen's compensation is highly organized, it has no government sanction and management is not obligated to provide this form of insurance for its employees. Participating organizations deposit funds which compensate for the death or permanent disability of employees according to requirements of the Ministry of Labor.

Agents and Brokers. The only legal regulations governing agents and brokers at the present time concerns commissions.

Social Insurance. The National Institute for Social Planning, a branch of the Ministry of Social Welfare, is in charge of social security. Obligatory life insurance for government officers and insurance for participants and attendants at sporting events are provided exclusively by the National Postal Savings Bank. The bank also participates in life and automobile insurance.

In the provinces where the Government Insurance Institute operates a branch office, it deals in either compulsory insurance lines or in the noncompulsory lines, competing with private insurance companies.

Reinsurance. INDER, the state-owned reinsurer, is the exclusive agent in the field of Reinsurance. Agencies of foreign groups have signed contracts for some risks that are not required to be covered by INDER. No national professional reinsurers are in business.

II. FORM AND OPERATION OF PRIVATE INSURERS

Basic Legal Rules. The basic legal rules are stated in the following: Code of Commerce, 5 October 1889; Law Number 11.672, 1943 edition, regarding the statute of the Insurance Supervisory Office; decree for the regulation of this law, 6 February 1939; decree regarding insurance company activities, 31 August 1961; decree regarding minimum stock, 13 October 1961, 7 February 1963, and 27 January 1967.

Legal Form. The above statutes concern stock companies, mutual and cooperative societies, and governmental entities (national, provincial, and municipal).

Social Purpose. Such purposes are limited exclusively to insurance and reinsurance operations and to the administration of those properties where their capital and reserves are invested.

Underwriting Authority. All types of operations are authorized provided the minimum capital requirements are met.

Constitutional Requirements. 1. Minimum Stock. In the case of national companies, the government states the rules for each case. In the case of foreign companies, the minimum capital required will be the same as for national companies. Any foreign company offering new lines must have capital and reserves equivalent to a minimum of 15% of the direct premiums.

2. Guaranty deposit. Only foreign companies are required to post this deposit, and the amount varies with the type of insurance. The deposit is

360,000 pesos for fire insurance and 180,000 pesos for all other types. A company providing two or more types of insurance deposits 120,000 pesos for all types after the first deposit. All deposits to the Argentinian National Bank are made in bonds representing the national public debt.

Process of Authorization. 1. Documentation. To receive authorization, a national company must submit a copy of the constitution and bylaws, insurance plans (structure, development, production), policies, rates, rating tables, powers and residence of the agents. In addition, foreign companies must produce documents written in the native language which prove they are authorized to operate in their homeland, plus headquarters' balance sheets for the past five years and any other materials the Insurance Commissioner may require.

2. Procedure. All records for national companies will be sent to the General Inspection of Juridical Entities, which issues a report concerning the bylaws. If they deal with cooperatives a report will be published by the National Department of Cooperatives of the Ministry of Social Welfare dealing with cooperatives.

The Supervisory Office then issues a report on structure and organization of the company, stressing its technical, administrative, and financial statutes.

All records and reports then are presented to the Ministry of the Treasury and Finance, and ultimately to the Ministry of Justice, which grants or denies the company the right to operate. The Supervisory Office gives authorization to begin operation when the right to operate has been granted. This authorization also must be recorded in the Register of Insurance Entities and published in the Official Bulletin.

Authorization is granted when the legal requisites have been fulfilled. An appeal to the Executive Power may be filed in case of denial.

Foreign companies follow the same procedure although the granting of a right to operate is discretionary. According to a decree of 11 June 1953, branches of foreign insurance companies may not be founded unless authorized by the Executive Power following a report from the National Reinsurance Institute and the Supervisory Office.

Reporting Obligations. National companies must forward to the Supervisory Office the balance sheet, annual report, and record of credit and debit within ten days from the time of approval by the Assembly. Foreign companies must submit the same documents within 180 days from the end of their fiscal year.

Companies selling life insurance must produce the following documents at least thirty days before the meeting of the Assembly: general report showing figures for its operations; new branches; premiums charged in the first year and their renewal; paid and outstanding claims; number of redemptions subscribed and policies rejected; accrued interests and rents on each class of goods representing mathematical, legal, optional reserves of capital; inventory

and general balance sheet of assets and liabilities with corresponding statement of profits and losses; and report to the auditor (not required for foreign
companies), or a report of the agent named by the company to represent it
before the Insurance Supervisory Office.

Balances will follow the pattern specified by the Supervisory Office (for
stock companies, or cooperatives and mutual societies), and they will be
published in the Official Bulletin.

III. CONTRACTING

Basic Legal Rules. These rules include the following: the Code of Com-
merce of 5 October 1889, decree of 6 February 1939, Aeronautical Code of 5
May 1967, edition 1943 of Law 11.672 regarding the legal statute of the
Insurance Supervisory Office, insurance law of 30 August 1967 substituting
Title VI of Book II of the Code of Commerce.

Policies. General conditions stated in the policies must be authorized by
the Supervisory Office, which must have a copy of the policies at least fifteen
days before the date proposed for its application. Supervisory Office approval
is required except in such special cases as Land and Passengers Transportation
Insurance and Marine Insurance. Usually the Insurance Companies Association suggests to the Supervisory Office standard wording of policies which are
binding in such fields as personal damages and specified diseases, automobile,
livestock, hailstorm, transport, glass, theft, fidelity, civil liability, fire, life,
marine, etc. Companies may apply for authorization of policies which are
different from the standard patterns.

Tariffs. Tariffs must be approved by the Supervisory Office. In the event
of administrative silence, new plans and tariffs are considered approved 120
working days after their introduction and existing plans 30 days after introduction.

Life insurance applications must be subscribed by an actuary. Applications
should include the tables and formulas used for determining risks, premiums,
reserves, guaranteed values and loadings. Tables of mortality and commuta-
tion should be included in cases of application for life insurance.

The Supervisory Office controls the premiums to avoid inadequacy, excesses, or arbitrary discrimination so that the market remains stable and
insurers solvent.

Compulsory Insurances. Personal accident insurance has been provided
attendants at sports events since 1953. The premium is included in the ticket
price. Other compulsory insurances are levied in some provinces, e.g., automobile third party liability in Misiones Province. This provision has been
enacted in the province of Buenos Aires but has not been enforced to date.

Insurance on all risks of the national government is required, including
decentralized departments and government-owned companies (excepting

stock companies, even when the government owns one hundred percent of its shares), as well as the Buenos Aires City Hall. According to a law of 14 December 1965, this insurance is carried through the National Postal Savings Bank. Life insurance on government officers must also be carried through this bank.

Private insurance in Argentina may be carried through any entity authorized to operate. An exception is the case of life insurance of government officers which must be covered by the National Postal Savings Bank. This bank is also authorized to contract insurance with provinces, municipalities, and mixed stock companies with respect to goods and interests.

Foreign Insurance Restrictions. Argentinian insurance (provided by companies founded and domiciled in Argentina and chartered by local authorities) is required for the following individuals and situations: persons, goods, or responsibilities of the nation, province, municipality, autonomous organizations or individuals (either judicial, business, or industrial) who hold permissions, franchises, exemptions or privileges of any kind where the receiver bears the risk of loss for the goods being imported or exported.

According to the law of 10 October 1971 marine insurance over imports from the United States attributed to the Alliance for Progress program may be contracted through Argentinian insurance companies by authorized marine insurance companies in the United States, provided the loan includes the financing of the insurance.

In most circumstances it is prohibited to insure with companies not established in Argentina. Failure to follow this practice will result in a fine equal to twenty-five times the premium if contracted inside the country.

IV. TECHNICAL RESERVES

Basic Legal Rules. The following basic rules apply: legal statute of the Supervisory Office 11.672, 1943 edition; Supervisory Office decisions of 23 September 1940 on the general statute for the constitution and restriction of reserves; 16 August 1951 creating a special reserve; 7 August 1953 on hailstorm loss; and 7 June 1956 on investment of reserves.

Classes. Mathematical calculation shall be made in accord with the technical notes approved by the Supervisory Office.

Under most circumstances premium reserves must be represented by 40% of the premiums for the fiscal year, omitting reinsurance and cancellations, although they may be calculated over the administrative charge with equal percentage and considering the same basis (Decision 3.854 and Collective Bargaining Agreement). In marine insurance, however, the total of the net premiums issued in the last two months of the fiscal year shall be reserved. In the cases of guaranty and fidelity insurance the 40% will be increased by an additional 15% over the average net premiums of the last three fiscal years. In passengers accident insurance the rule will be 15% of the net premiums. However, if the Supervisory Office deems that the relation between risks and reserves is not satisfactory, it may establish other procedures, such as the method of the "twenty-fourths," given the fact that any company has considerably increased its production in the last months of the fiscal year.

All reserves must be invested in Argentina. Under most circumstances, reserves should be invested in the following manner: (1) securities or bonds, either national, provincial, or municipal; (2) public foreign bonds up to the amount of the mathematical reserves corresponding to the policies issued in such foreign currencies, whenever international reciprocity is admitted; (3) specially secured obligations whenever the goods are established in Argentina, including mortgage loans; real estate; shares of Argentinian stock companies or foreign companies engaged in public services in Argentina; loans warranted with certificates, obligations, or shares; loans with banking endorsements.

Reserves must be kept independently for life insurance and various other branches of insurance by an amount sufficient to pay the cost of compensation plus any corresponding expenses. Hailstorm Loss Reserve is singled out as most obligatory for companies operating in this branch. This reserve is formed with the 20% of the profits from the branch until it reaches 100% of the premiums of direct insurance and active reinsurance (excepting the premiums of contracts in excess of loss and retrocession of the National Reinsurance Institute, omitting cancellations and passive reinsurances) of the fiscal year where this sum was larger during the past five years. This reserve may be used only when losses exceed 60% of premiums of direct insurance and accepted reinsurance, omitting cancellations and outward reinsurances, with a limit of 50% of the reserves in one fiscal year.

The reserve for fluctuation of values is called "reserve for devaluation of investments," or the "reserve for fluctuation of public bonds." To estimate it, the following issues must be added: (1) profits resulting from the sale of surrender of bonds and (2) the largest amount resulting from computing the 10% of net annual profits or the 0.5% of the inventory value of the existing certificates.

There is also the so-called "Resolution 2190 Special Reserve" of a general character, that is formed with the percentages of the profits of every fiscal year over the sum of the capital plus reserves, as specified: (1) 12.5% of such profits, when the profits are between 5 and 10% of that sum; (2) 25% when the profits are between 15 and 25%; (3) 50% when the profits are over 15%. After applying these rules, profits that exceed 20% of the addition of capital plus reserves must be imputed also. Other special reserves that may be quoted are those corresponding to real estate, devaluation of shares and debentures, devaluations of shares to be reimbursed, self-gotten shares, loans (from several classes), debt under contingencies, etc.

General Requirements of Goods To Be Used as Reserve Covers.   Securities must meet certain requirements to be accepted as legal reserves. In the case of public funds guaranteed by provinces and municipalities, obligations without special guarantees, stock company shares, and loans guaranteed by securities, the issuing company must fulfill the following prerequisites: (1) the company must be up to date in the payment of the amortization, interest or dividend of all bonds at the time of purchase; (2) payments should have been regular during the past seven years; (3) companies must enjoy a prestige of well-known solvency when they intend to invest shares or obligations; (4) shares must be quoted in the stock exchange and the company should have paid a dividend of at least 5% during the past seven years. In special cases the Supervisory Office may admit the investment of bonds, shares or obligations although the seven-year term is not met.

Investment in speculative values is not permitted. For instance, real estate investments must be in Argentina. Mortgage loans are accepted only if they have a first lien on real estate located in Argentina. Foreign countries' public bonds are accepted if reciprocity with bonds of the national public debt is obligatory.

General Limits of Investment. Maximum and minimum limits of investment exist. Life insurance companies are submitted to special quotas according to the following rules:

Securities	General percentage of total investment	Life insurance companies
1. Bonds and income public securities	25% min.	10%
2. Real estate and mortgage loans	together: 60% max.	80%
	individual:40% max.	50%
3. Other securities	15% max.	20%
(Forestation Co. shares)	25% max.	30%
Individually the sum of the forestation shares, as much as the other investments, cannot exceed	15%	20%

A decree of October 1961 established the obligation of investing a minimum of 50% of the reserves and the constitution special funds in housing bonds, but this has not been enforced. Investments in shares or obligation of a company or group of companies cannot exceed the 20% of the total issued by them or 10% of the issuing company of an insurance company. A minimum of 25% of the investments must be in government securities (10% in life insurance companies).

The statute of investments for cooperative and mutual societies is similar to that of the stock company. In addition they can invest in shares of like societies whenever they have a surplus of cover. The maximum investment may not exceed 10% of the reserves of the issuing company and those of the buying entity.

V. REINSURANCE

Basic Legal Rules.   Law 12.988 of 13 October 1952 sets up the National Reinsurance Institute (INDER); the decree of 9 July 1953 contains its organizational statute. The decree of 11 June 1953 rearranges the text of the 1947 reinsurance law.

Characteristics of the Present Statute. Reinsurance in the following branches of insurance is monopolized by INDER: life, transport (cargo and hulls), fire, hailstorm, automobile, contractor's risks, aviation, and personal accidents. The remaining lines have freedom of reinsurance.

Argentinian insurance companies must cede to the Institute all excesses of their own retentions (to be determined by each company. INDER also demands some minimum retention, according to the acknowledgement of the ceding company, in cases of bad loss, such as automobile, theft, etc.). Companies whose capital and management are not rooted in Argentina must cede to INDER no less than 30% of all risks contracted in Argentina, plus the percentage of the rest that INDER may establish. The remaining excess will be arranged for such companies.

The Institute may authorize the companies for direct reinsurance even in foreign countries, if it is impossible or inconvenient to accept the risk because of the nature of the risk or the condition of the market.

Cessions and excesses received by the Institute will be retroceded to national insurers preferably, once self-retention is deducted. If any excess remains, it may be retroceded to other non-national markets or to foreign companies. Reciprocity may be utilized when it seems convenient to the Institute.

The basic goal of INDER, according to its organizational statute, is the protection of public interest of insurance companies and its equitable redistribution among Argentinian companies, remembering their positions as ceding or accepting entities. INDER normally gives the same commissions on business accepted from retrocessionaires and charges loading for the administration and distribution of the reinsurance contract.

Argentinian companies subscribing to reinsurance contracts, especially on risks not handled by INDER, must notify the Insurance Supervisory Office to this effect.

Insurance companies may accept only the reinsurance cessions or retrocessions related to those branches in which the Supervisory Office has authorized them to have direct operations. When operating in branches other than those authorized, they must have special authorization from the office and must fulfill a series of requirements for that purpose.

VI. TAXES

Basic Legal Rules. The basic laws governing taxes include law number 11.682 regarding revenue tax and unified internal taxes; law number 14.060 regarding the tax that substitutes the assessment of free transmission of goods; and law number 11.582 of 10 April 1934 regarding internal taxes.

Premium Taxes and Loadings. Five types of taxes fall into this category: (1) Internal Taxes (unified, federal, and provincial). The rate for patrimonial risks is 8.5% and for workmen's compensation is 2.5%. Life and personal accidents are exempted. (2) Seal Taxes. These have a federal character and apply on policies issued in the national capital. When the insured risk or person lives in a province, the federal tax takes precedence over the local one. The rate for patrimonial risks is usually 1%; life and personal accidents are exempted. (3) Supervisory Office Rate. This is equivalent to 5% of the total premiums charged on all branches. (4) Social Services Rate for Personnel. This is 5% of the total of premiums charged in all branches; life is exempted. (5) Administrative Loading. These vary from 21 to 35% of the premiums.

Income Taxes and Loadings. Income tax is the only charge on profits. The rate is 33% on profits for companies constituted outside Argentina and 8% over dividends or profits produced inside Argentina.

VII. PRODUCTION (AGENTS)

Basic Legal Rules. Basic laws for agencies include Decree 8312 of 1942 and various resolutions of the Supervisory Office for the periodical establishment of fees.

Kinds of Agents. Technically speaking, there are three kinds of agents. (1) dependent producers, who are professionals and are affiliated with a particular insurance company (exclusive agents); (2) independent producers, who are also professionals but who have no exclusive link with a particular company (independent agents); (3) occasional independent producers, who have no relationship with any particular company and deal in insurance as a sideline.

For practical purposes another classification is sometimes used: agents are ordinary salesmen; organizing agents work in urban areas; country organizers work in rural areas; superintendents, organize agents dealing only in life insurance; production directors, are life insurance producers affiliated with only one company.

Societies of insurance brokers are recognized legally as a group and their members as individual agents.

Previous Requirements. For all practical purposes each company hires its own agents, who have no legal prerequisite.

Authorization. No process has been established for an official authorization for professional activity. Law 11.672 mentions the establishment of a Life Insurance Agents Register controlled by the Supervisory Office and the obligation of insurance companies to operate through agents listed in this Register, but neither rule has been effectively enforced to date.

Bail. There is no obligation for bonds or other kinds of security deposits. Insurance companies are responsible for their agents and their behavior and activities.

Agency Contracts. The contract designating an individual as agent of a company is considered as a mandate.

There is no relation between the labor contract and the standard pattern for the agency contract. The only conditions are the market's "practices and rules" that define the basic rights of the agent.

Commissions. The Supervisory Office, considering the market conditions of the time that the premium rate is set, establishes the rate of commissions for compulsory insurance. The agent is entitled to some additional percentages, which are calculated on the production obtained by his salesmen and determined by the Supervisory Office.

Official Protection. The Insurance Agents Association (APAS) offers free membership for all kinds of agents; one of its principal goals is the enacting of an agents' statute. There are no incompatibilities established legally. Producers, either dependent or independent, have social security protection and, therefore, are affiliated with the Retirement Bank. Thus they receive an annual complementary payment proportional to the commissions charged. Portfolio rights are not regulated.

VIII. INSTITUTIONAL BODIES

Governmental Entities. These include the following:

1. National Insurance Supervisory Office (SSN), which is an autonomous entity within the Ministry of the Treasury and Finance. Its basic function is to control insurance activities within the country with its ramifications, economical and technical. Thus it supervises the organization, operation, financial standing, and liquidation of insurance societies, either private, governmental, or mixed. It especially supervises plans, premiums, contract forms, balance sheets, intermediary systems, publicity and promotion.

The Executive Power, through the Ministry of the Treasury and the Supervisory Office, determines the minimum capital required for insurance activities. A body of inspectors is in charge of external control of insurance activities.

2. Consultative Board, which is a consulting body associated with the Supervisory Office and concerned with the following tasks: (1) when requested by the superintendent, it issues reports about bills, decrees or bylaws concrening insurance activities or intermediaries; bookkeeping, balance and statistics systems; policies and uniform tariffs; annual fees for the Supervisory Office; expenses; and serious breaches of laws; (2) submits to the superintendent proposals concerning improvement of the insuring entity; (3) reports on relevant insurance affairs.

The board is comprised of five directors selected by proposal of the following entities: (1) two by stock companies who have been legally recognized by the Executive Power; (2) one by stock companies recognized by the provincial government; (3) one by either one or the other group of companies; and (4) one by agencies or branch offices of foreign companies.

3. Mutuals and Cooperatives Consultative Committee, which is a consultative group affiliated with the Supervisory Office for aiding in insurance cooperatives and mutual societies affairs. It consists of five persons appointed by the superintendent from a list prepared by mutual societies and cooperatives.

4. National Reinsurance Institute (INDER) is a government company concerned with control and distribution of the reinsurance business. It is affiliated with the Ministry of the Treasury and Finance, and its key purposes include the following: (1) To function in reinsurance activities. It may formalize agreements, sign contracts, or deal with any other national or foreign institutions, insurance, or reinsurance societies. (2) To study the conditions of the Argentinian insurance market and to establish policies for the national economy regarding the international market, with the guidance of the Ministry of Finance. (3) To propose the establishment of new insurance branches. When national companies do not assume coverage of certain risks, it may operate as direct insurer. (4) To keep the Executive Power informed on all affairs connected with insurance in the nation.

INDER's capital, fixed by a decree of 10 September 1971 at twenty million pesos, and reserves are to be invested in real estate, public securities, and mortgage credits. INDER is governed by a board comprised of a president, one vice-president, and three directors. The directors are the superintendent of insurance and two deputies of the Ministry of Finance. The president and vice-president are nominated by the Executive Power.

5. National Postal Savings Bank was created in 1946 to insure government property and operate in nearly all branches of insurance.

6.. Government Aviation Insurance Company is an organization that covers the risks and responsibilities of the national airways companies, mixed capital companies and government subsidized private entities.

7. Other Governmental Bodies. The most important additional govern-

mental bodies are the Autonomous Insurance Institute of Entre Ríos, the Popular Savings Bank of Tucumán, and the Provincial Insurance Institutes of Salta and Misiones.

Associations.   These include the following:

1. Argentinian Association of Insurance Companies, which was founded 20 July 1894 and its charter was granted by a decree of 9 March 1946. It is composed of national stock companies dealing in insurance, and on 30 December 1970 it had 149 associated companies. It has two main purposes: (1) to promote the prestige of the insurance business and (2) to promote better relations with governmental groups associated with insurance activities. The Assembly of its partners, is its highest authority which, in turn, appoints a ruling board to administer its activities. The president and a limited number of members of the board constitute the executive committee which governs the association.

2. Argentinian Foreign Insurers Association, which was founded in 1875, and it represents foreign companies operating in Argentina. It supports their common interests and assists them as trade organization both in taxes and legal affairs. It is directed by a president and vice-president appointed by the assembly and an executive commission composed of deputies appointed by companies of all branches. The commission has nine members plus the president and vice-president. Fire, Accident, and Transport constitute separate internal branches. This association plus the Argentinian Association of Insurance Companies constitutes the Insurers Chamber.

3. Argentinian Association of Insurance Cooperatives and Mutual Societies, which was founded on 1 November 1940 and chartered on 23 November 1945, was declared a representative entity of its members by a National Insurance Supervisory Office resolution on 23 November 1953. Its purposes are to cooperate with governmental officers in the field of mutual insurance, promote special legislation regarding cooperative and mutual insurance, and to increase integration among these groups. It also publishes their principles. The association is comprised of cooperative and mutual societies established according to its rules and bylaws. The Directive Commission is composed of nine members and five substitutes. Forty-six entities belong to the association.

4. Insurance Workers Trade Union, which is in charge of promoting better working conditions among insurance, reinsurance, and saving and loans company workers. It also assists them with collective bargaining. Affiliation is not required.

5. Insurance Agents and Producers Association, which was founded 27 August 1959 for brokers who operate as intermediaries between clients and insurance companies. It attempts to improve the technical capabilities of its members, giving them better status in the profession and contributing to a larger national insurance market and better understanding. The association publishes an important magazine on insurance and offers courses in the

subject. A statute of the insurance producer has been submitted to the National Supervisory Office which would regulate the producer's rights and duties, and establish his responsibilities and working conditions.

6. Actuary Institute, which was formed on 16 October 1949 as the Argentinian Actuary Institute, following the work begun by the Argentinian Institute of Actuaries organized in 1919. It is composed of a board and the general assembly. It has six directors, and the members of the assembly serve in either an active or passive function. Its purpose is the affiliation of professional actuaries.

7. Argentinian Association of Insurance Law, which is a national branch of AIDA International. Its members are outstanding professors, attorneys, actuaries, bookkeepers, and insurers who study and promote insurance law.

8. Professional Insurance School, which is an institution, with headquarters in Buenos Aires, that provides professional training for insurance company workers. It is affiliated with the Argentinian Association of Insurance Companies.

9. Argentine University of Management (UADE), is an institution that grants a degree or license in insurance after four years of study plus a doctoral degree for another year of study.

10. Insurance Studies and Research Center (CEIS) was organized by the Hemispheric Insurance Conference to provide technical studies in insurance.

IX. CHARACTERISTICS OF THE SIXTIES

Insurance Contract Ruling. Law 17.418 regulating insurance contracts and wording of general conditions of the policies was enacted on 30 July 1967. A project regarding the statute of insurance companies and their control was prepared in the same year, now under study by the Executive Power.

Automobile Insurance Development. Automobile insurance premiums on elementary branches has grown from 27.7% to 66% between 1960 and 1970.

Inflation. The negative influence of the inflationary trend has affected insurance activity.

Scientific Work. An interest has developed during this decade towards the study of subjects related to insurance. Specialized congresses and seminars such as the Second Panamerican Congress on Insurance Law met in Buenos Aires in November 1969. On 22 December 1960 the Argentinian branch of the Association Internationale de Droit des Assurances (AIDA) (International Association of Insurance Law) was organized, and the charter was granted on 11 July 1963. Several meetings connected with insurance subjects are promoted by this association. The Panamerican Congress is one of its top activities.

Other Aspects. In 1963 rules were promulgated which establish differential statutes on foreign and Argentinian companies on the basis of the nationality of stockholders and directors. Tax exemptions for insurance cooperatives were modified in the same year.

Law 17.051 passed in 1966 establishes rules for funeral expenses insurance. Decree 528/67 sets the minimum stocks required for the constitution of insurance entities. Law 17.145, enacted in the same year, eliminates the necessity for making and publishing a balance of insurance entities every three months.

Through a resolution of the Insurance Supervisory Office, the Insurance Division of the National Postal Savings Bank was put under the official control of the public treasury.

The requirements of the policies of Guarantee Insurance were set on 31 January 1969. Export credit insurance was modified on April 21, thus authorizing the coverages of manufacture and credit risks. The Insurance Assessing Commission, composed of insurers, producers, and employees' deputies, was also organized in 1969. Its function is to study the modernization of rules regarding the operation of insurance companies.

X. FUNDAMENTAL LEGISLATION

Chronological Order

4 August 1927—Decree of bookkeeper and balance sheet, No. 4.

6 February 1939—Regulatory decree on legal system of insurance company, No. 23.350.

26 April 1940—Decree on Consultative Board, No. 61.138.

19 August 1940—Decree on foreign agencies' inscription, No. 67.185.

23 Sept. 1940—Resolution about premium reserve, No. 124.

27 June 1941—Resolution on general rules of evaluation, No. 193.

1943 Edition—Law No. 11.672 on legal system of the Supervisory Office.

10 July 1947—Resolution on report system of foreign companies, No. 1.020.

7 February 1949—Resolution on foreign companies' system, No. 1.523.

26 January 1950—Resolution on elimination of "policy rights", No. 1801.

5 May 1952—Resolution on agents' commissions, No. 2.362.

22 May 1952—Resolution regarding insurers' associations, No. 2.388.

25 June 1952—Resolution on agents' commissions, No. 2.419.

20 October 1952—Constitutive law of National Reinsurance Institute, No. 12.988.

9 July 1953—Decree on organizing statute of the Reinsurance National Institute, No. 10.073.

7 August 1953—Resolution on reserves covering major hailstorm loss, No. 2.644.

7 August 1953—Resolution on air navigation and hailstorm insurances, No. 2.643.

29 September 1953—Resolution regarding cooperative and mutual societies and insurance company associations, No. 2.693.

7 September 1954—Resolution on fire risks reserve, No. 3.099.

1 September 1955—Resolution on organizing agency, No. 3.386.

27 December 1955—Resolution on special reserve, No. 2.180.

3 February 1956—Resolution on organization, competence and operation of the Insurance Supervisory Office, No. 3.472.

18 May 1956—Resolution on minimum stocks, No. 3.507.

4 February 1957—Resolution on mutual and cooperative societies, No. 3.634.

7 February 1957—Resolution on mutual and cooperative societies, No. 3.634.

5 July 1957—Resolution on marine insurance of INDER, No. 3.678.

29 December 1959—Law on mutual and cooperatives societies, No. 15.026.

25 July 1960—Resolution on loans and advances system, No. 4.591.

13 October 1961—Decree on national stock companies and foreign companies, No. 9.167.

13 October 1961—Decree on "housing bonds" investment, No. 9.168.

12 June 1962—Decree on national stock companies and foreign companies, No. 5.366.

25 October 1962—Resolution on investment and lending societies, No. 5.896.

30 August 1967—Insurance law that substitutes Title VI of Book 2 of Commerce Code.

By Subject

Legal system for the insurance company—law No. 11.672 on legal system of the Insurance Supervisory Office, Edition 1943; regulatory decree, 6 February 1939; insurance law that substitutes Title VI, Book 2 of Commerce Code, 30 August 1967.

Complementary legal rules—(minimum stocks): law on mutual and cooperative societies, 29 December 1959; decree on national stock companies and foreign companies, 13 October 1961; idem, 12 June 1940; (consultative board): decree about operation, 26 April 1940; (investments): decree on "Housing bonds" investments, 13 October 1961; (operating system): decree about balance sheet and bookkeeping, 4 August 1927; decree on inscription of foreign agencies, 19 August 1940.

General rules of the Supervisory Office—(constitution, development and operations): resolution on reporting system of foreign companies, 10 July 1947; idem on minimum stocks, 18 May 1956; (reserves): resolutions on premium reserves, 23 September 1940; idem on major hailstorm loss reserves, 7 August 1953; idem on fire risks reserves, 7 September 1954; idem on resolution 2.190 special reserve, 27 December 1955; (investments): resolution on general rules of evaluation, 27 June 1941; idem on foreign companies' system, 7 February 1949; idem on mutual and cooperative societies system, 4 February 1957; idem on loans and advancements system, 25 August 1960;

idem on furnishing societies investment, 25 October 1962; (policies and rates): resolution on elimination of the "right of policy," 26 January 1950; idem regarding insurers' associations, 22 May 1952; idem regarding mutual and cooperative insurance companies' associations, 29 September 1953; idem on procedure for the approval of new rates, 7 February 1956; (commissions): resolution on producers' fees, 5 May 1952; idem, 25 June 1952; idem on organizing agencies, 1 September 1955; (retrocessions of INDER): resolution on hailstorm and air navigation branches, 7 August 1953; idem on marine insurance, 5 July 1957.

Insurance Supervisory Office—resolution on organization competence and operation, 3 February 1956.

Reinsurance National Institute—organizing law, 20 October 1952; decree on organizing law, 9 July 1953.

Bolivia

I. GENERAL INFORMATION

Historical Note. The first stage in the history of Bolivian insurance included both the colonial period and the beginning of the republic. At that time policies did not exist and metal cargoes were insured through "notarial contracts."

La Previsora, an Argentinian company, was the first authorized to establish life insurance agency in Bolivia. Bankruptcy of the mother company caused the dissolution of this agency. La Sudamericana, a branch of a Chilean company, was established in 1908. Therefore Bolivian insurance begins only in the middle of this century when La Boliviana de Seguros was founded in 1946.

Official Control. According to a decree of 28 October 1970, control is granted to the Control Division of the Central Bank. Formerly the Bank Supervisory Office had this responsibility.

Professional Management. The Bolivian Insurers Association is representative of the majority of the companies. It provides a guild-like representation of Bolivian insurers.

Market Structure. The market is formed by thirteen general insurance companies, a life insurance company, and three companies providing mixed insurance. Bolivian companies collect more than twice as much insurance premiums as foreign agencies in the country. The most important branches include fire, transport, employee bail, personal accident, aviation, automobile, third party liability, fulfillment of contract, and life.

International Expansion. Has no special importance in Bolivia.

Workmen's Compensation. This is included in Social Security. This is required and is administered under the National Compulsory Social Security Fund created by law 14 December 1956 (Social Security Code).

Agents and Brokers. Regulation of agents and brokers is limited; they operate incidentally in insurance operations at present.

Public Insurance. With the exception of the required Social Security which embraces all public and private organizations, estates insurances of official or private companies have to be contracted with private insurers. Some insurance offices, such as railroad and bank employees' offices, operate independently.

Reinsurance. There is little international reinsurance. When it exists it operates without restriction in all private insurance companies by either treaty or free agreement.

II. FORM AND OPERATION OF PRIVATE INSURERS

Basic Legal Rules. These laws include the one of 27 September 1904 concerning the composition of insurance companies, the Supreme Decree (enforceable as a law) of 3 August 1962 concerning minimum capital of insurance companies, the law of 13 November 1886 concrening the legal system of stock companies, and the Commerce Code of 1865. The former Bank Supervisory Office and the Bolivian Insurers Association have prepared two projects on insurance law providing for review and coordination by the executive power.

Judicial Nature. Insurance activities may be conducted only through authorized corporations.

Social Purposes. These are limited exclusively to the operations of insurance and reinsurance.

Scope of Operations. If minimum capital requirements are fulfilled, a company may operate in all insurance lines.

Constitutional Requirements. Both national and foreign companies are required to deposit 500,000,000 Bolivian pesos to operate in either life insurance or in general risks; companies operating in both kinds of insurance simultaneously must deposit 750,000,000 pesos. Capital must be totally subscribed and disimbursed.

Both Bolivian and foreign companies must deposit a warrant of 30,000 Bolivian pesos (in securities) although this warrant may be included in the minimum capital required, according to a resolution of 27 July 1966 from the Bank Supervisory Office.

Process of Authorization. As a prerequisite to achieving authorization Bolivian companies must submit the constitution of a stock company, the subscription and disbursement of all social stock, a list of members of the board or directory of administration, and proof that the company is legally recognized by the executive power through a supreme resolution. Subsequently the Bolivian Central Bank Control Division authorizes the operation of a company so that it may begin operation. Foreign companies must prove that they are legally established in their home countries and must deposit in Bolivia the minimum stock which is required of Bolivian companies. They must also nominate a trustee or legal representative to act on their behalf.

Reporting Obligations. Bolivian companies must send an annual report of profits and losses and monthly reports of production to the Control Division of the Central Bank within thirty days following the end of each month or year that they are due. Foreign Companies must send, in addition to the above, the annual report of the headquarters companies.

III. CONTRACTING

Basic Legal Rules. These include the law for insurance companies of 27 September 1904, the law on required contracting which must be made by government institutions in national or foreign companies of 29 September 1968.

Policies. General conditions of policies are regulated by the Control Division of the Central Bank. Because there is no specific law in insurances, the rules of civil and commerce codes state that policies constitute a contract between parties. The general conditions are normally based on policies used in European and North American markets.

Tariffs. Tariffs are obligatory for all member companies and they may be approved through agreements by the Bolivian Association of Insurers. Minimum tariffs must be approved by the control division of the Central Bank.

Required Insurance. Compulsory contracts include workmen's compensation, which is included in Social Security and depends on government monies, and fire insurance for creditors, which is required to obtain a mortgage or pledge loan.

In addition, a law of 29 September 1928 states that companies in which the government has an economic interest, and which need to be insured, must subscribe to insurance in national companies or foreign agencies established in Bolivia.

Restrictions on Foreign Insurance. The covering of risks in foreign countries is forbidden, according to a law of 27 September 1904, unless authorized by the Bank Supervisory Office. This authorization is granted only when it is proved that the type of insurance required is not feasible in companies legally established in Bolivia. Companies engaging in clandestine insurance coverage are fined 31% of their premiums if discovered. It is also forbidden to provide risks in foreign territories with respect to (1) persons domiciled in the territory of the republic, (2) property or any other kind of insurable item of national jurisdiction, (3) goods transported to or from the country when risks are to be borne by persons domiciled in the country, and (4) vehicles, ships, and planes with national registration.

IV. TECHNICAL RESERVES

Basic Legal Rules. These include the following: the law of 27 September 1904 on the technical reserve system; the resolution of 1 April 1964 on reserve investment; and the Supreme Decree of 26 March 1917 on cancellation of deposits.

Classses. The determination of the mathematical classes for life insurance is according to mortality tables approved by the Bank Supervisory Office. The type of interest cannot exceed an annual 6%.

All reserves must be invested on Bolivian territory. A minimum of 80% of all mathematical reserves and current risks must be invested in (1) bonds or public titles, (2) corporation shares, (3) loans to commercial and industrial enterprises, (4) urban real estate for rent, (5) mortgage bills of exchange, (6) private loans warranted with first mortgage on real estates, (7) loans on life insurance policies, (8) loans to stock securities subscribers, and (9) mortgage participation contracts. The remaining 20% may be invested any way the company chooses.

The required reserve consists of the average total reserve of the valid policies existing at the end of each fiscal year. Premium reserves are made up of 40% of the premiums of the fiscal year, with the previous discount of reinsurances and annulments.

The calculation of outstanding losses is made annually on the basis of the amount of pending payments.

General Requirements of Goods to be Used as Reserve Covers. Stock company shares may be used in this category only if they belong to companies domiciled in Bolivia and if their investments are in the republic. Loans to industrial and commercial companies are to be backed up with mortgage or pledge warranty exceeding at least 40% of the value of the credit. Urban real estates are approved if they are located in Bolivia and are insured against fire risks.

Mortgage bills of exchange are approved, but interests from mortgage banks operating in Bolivia must be used. Private loans covering the first mortgage on real estate are approved if the real estate is located in Bolivia. Loans on life insurance policies are approved, but their values must be approved according to respective technical plans. Contracts of mortgage shares may be used if they are insured by the Central Housing Saving and Loans Fund by credits granted by mutual associations.

General Limits of Investment. Limitations include the following: (1) Private loans warranted on the first mortgage cannot exceed 60% of the value of the mortgaged real estate. (2) Investments in certificates made in favor of one person, entity, or firm cannot exceed 25% of the total invested reserves. (3) Investment on mathematical reserves may be made on periods up to five years, but semestral renewals are required. For plans involving loans to the insured, the interest of the loans for different life insurance plans cannot exceed 0.5% monthly. (4) Reserves for current risks and those retained for reinsurers can be invested in short term obligations (up to three years to maturity) with quarterly renewals; interest on these loans will be at the current bank rate: 15% annually.

V. REINSURANCE

Basic Legal Rules. None exist in this field.

Judicial Nature. Legally, reinsurance is handled through stock corporations.

Process of Authorization. This process is the same as that for companies operating in direct insurance. No special demand exists for foreign insurers which are not domiciled in Bolivia.

Reporting Obligations. National companies must report to the control department of the Central Bank regarding any change, substitution, or cancellation of their reinsurance contracts. Foreign companies must prove their reinsurance operations legally so that their profits and loss accounts may be considered.

Remnants and Remittances in Foreign Currency. A check in foreign currency imbursed to the Central Bank will be required. When local companies charge the premiums in dollars, remittances must be made with their own funds.

Government Control. This is provided by the control department of the Central Bank, which assumes all functions previously granted the Bank Supervisory Office, according to a decree of 28 October 1970. In most instances there are no restrictions for reinsurers, whether they are Bolivian or foreign. Contracts between ceding companies and reinsurers is binding for both parties.

VI. TAXES

Basic Legal Rules. These include the decree of 30 October 1951 regarding contributions of insurance companies to the insurance department of the Bank Supervisory Office; the law of 4 February 1958 on stamps for insurance policies; the Supreme Decree of 23 February 1957 establishing the tax on sales, services, and insurance premiums.

Taxes and Loadings over Premiums. A 3% premium tax is levied on all types of insurance except life insurance. A 4% stamp tax is levied on the collected premiums. All insurance companies are required to contribute 3% of the net premiums collected for the maintenance of the insurance department of the Bank Supervisory Office.

Taxes and Loadings over Profits. Insurance companies are required to produce a statement of profit sharing immediately after its approval by the general meeting of stockholders or the board, according to their laws or regulations. This must be presented to the control division. The tax on profits is 25%.

Other Taxes.   These include (1) a tax on losses, which is equivalent to 1% of all losses paid to the person insured or to the damaged or beneficiary, (2) a municipal register, which is equivalent to 1.5% on the capital and reserves of insurance companies, and (3) a tax on commissions. Registered commissioned agents must pay 8%; those who have no authorized registration must pay 16%.

VII. PRODUCTION (AGENTS)

Basic Legal Rule.   This is the resolution of 12 February 1963, stemming from the supreme decree of 12 March 1949 regarding the listing of agents in the official register. It regulates the operations of private insurance agents.

Kinds of Agents.   Agents are listed as life insurance agents, diverse branches agents, insurance agents in general, and sales agents.

Previous Requirements.   An agent must be recognized legally, he must be listed in the Insurance and Capitalization Register, and he must have passed a test which proves his capacity to operate in his particular insurance field.

Authorization.   Agents must be authorized by the Bank Supervisory Office. This authorization may be requested by the company using the agent's services or by the agent himself. The agent can negotiate his documentation at the control office of the Central Bank.

Authorization will be granted after the agent proves he has sufficient knowledge in private insurance and capitalization. The agent must take an examination at the insurance department of the Bank Supervisory Office. Approved candidates will be authorized by a resolution and they will be registered under a number which should appear on the credential given by the company in which the agent works.

Bail.   Bail is not required.

Agency Contracts.   These contracts are negotiated directly between the company and the agent; conditions and limitations of representation are stated in the contract.

Retribution Commissions.   Companies will pay commissions to properly authorized agents only. Agent commissions should not be paid on insurance contracts where the agent has not participated or in the case of state insurance adjudgment by contests. When commissions are not paid, it must be indicated that agents were not involved. The only exception to this rule is that commissions are paid to recognized brokerage companies. Normal commissions include the following: fire, transport, personal accident—15%; automobile—10%; life—60% the first year, 30% the second year, and 10% the third year.

Official Protection.   Public officials in general and companies or persons owning insured interests may not act as agents. Officials and employees of the fiscal department of the Central Bank and managers, assistant managers, proxies, administrators and other executives and salaried employees of insurance companies may not be listed in the Agents Register. Portfolio rights are transferable under conditions established by agency contracts.

VIII. INSTITUTIONAL BODIES

Governmental Entities. By a law of 28 October 1970 the fiscal division assumes the duties corresponding to the bank superintendency. The primary function of this division is to control insurance operations and establish general guidelines. This division also grants authorization for establishing new insurance companies.

The professional organ of this division is comprised of representatives of the Confederation of Private Entrepeneurs of Bolivia, the Bolivian Insurers Association, and the president of the National Chamber of Commerce. It does not necessarily function as an arbitration group.

Associations. The majority of the insurance companies in Bolivia are associated with the Bolivian Association of Insurers.

IX. CHARACTERISTICS OF THE SIXTIES

In 1962, by supreme law-decree, norms were established for the constitution of minimum capital for insurance corporations. In 1963 the decree of March 12, 1949 was enforced and the functions of private insurance agents were regulated. In 1964 norms were established on the investment of technical reserves. In 1970, by law-decree, the general control of insurance production fell under the fiscal division of the banking superintendent.

X. FUNDAMENTAL LEGISLATION

Chronological Order

13 November 1886—law on legal control of stock companies.

27 September 1904—law on the constitution of insurance companies and technical reserves rule.

26 March 1917—supreme decree on cancellation of deposits.

12 March 1949—supreme decree on listing insurance agents in the Official Register.

30 October 1951—Law-decree on the contribution of insurance companies to the maintenance of the insurance department of the Banking Superintendent.

3 August 1962—supreme decree-law on minimum capital of insurance companies.

12 February 1963—resolution enforced by the 12 March 1949 decree regulating functions of private insurance agents.

1 April 1964—resolution on investment of reserves.

29 September 1968—law on required contracting by state institutions in national companies or foreign agencies.

28 October 1970—decree-law establishing the functions of fiscalization of the banking superintendent.

By Subject

General dispositions—(1) law on legal control of corporations, 13 November 1886, (2) law on formation of insurance companies and technical reserves rule, 27 September 1904, (3) supreme decree on cancellation of deposits, 26 March 1917, (4) supreme decree-law on minimum capital for insurance companies, 3 August 1962, (5) resolution on investment of reserves, 1 April 1964, (6) decree-law establishing functions of the fiscalization division of the banking superintendent, 28 October 1970.

Agents—(1) Supreme decree on listing insurance agents in the Official Register, 12 March 1949, and (2) resolution with ruling on the former decree and regulation of private agents' functions, 12 November 1963.

Required Contracting—Law on required contracting which must be carried out by state institutions in national insurance companies or foreign agencies, 29 September 1968.

Other Dispositions—decree-law on the contribution of insurance companies to the maintenance of the insurance department of the banking superintendent, 30 October 1951.

Brazil

I. GENERAL INFORMATION

Historical Note. The first insurance company, Boa Fe, was established in Bahía in February 1806, and it dealt in marine insurance. The first Brazilian mutual insurance society was organized in 1828. In 1845 a transport insurance company called Argus Fluminense began operations in marine insurance.

The first foreign companies, English or Portuguese, were established in the decade of 1860–1970. During this period legislation regulating insurance activities was enacted. These laws required an authorization for operating in the market, the approval of social statutes, and the production of balance sheets.

The first structural bylaw and the organization of the Insurance General Supervisory Office as a government control office took place at the beginning of the twentieth century. In April 1939 the Reinsurance Institute of Brazil was established.

Official Control. The Ministry of Industry and Commerce exercises government control of insurance through the Private Insurance National Board which, in turn, acts through the Private Insurance Superintendency.

Professional Statute. Professional insurers have their maximum representation in the Sindicatos Nacionales de Entidades Aseguradores. It is a part of the National Federation of Private Insurance and Stock Companies. Insurance brokers are organized in regional syndicates.

Both kinds of institutions represent and defend associates' interests before government agencies. They also maintain a state of fair competition inside their territories.

Market Structure. Private insurance in Brazil operates exclusively through stock corporations (184 in all). The few mutual societies which existed previously have disappeared. Five companies control 25% of the market. The stock of some of these companies is controlled by states of the federation.

In many cases the existing companies operate in groups. The actual policy of the government is to strengthen the insurance market by encouraging mergers. The granting authorization for insurance companies has been suspended during the past three years. Minimum stock requirements have been increased gradually, and companies which are in the process of merging have been entitled to special financial privileges.

International Expansion. Not only has international expansion progressed remarkably in the past few years, but there is also an increasing trend to widen relations with foreign markets.

Workmen's Compensation. Workmen's compensation is regulated by law-decrees of 10 November 1944 and 13 May 1945. Loss prevention organizations, insurance societies, cooperatives and pension funds were authorized to operate in this field in 1953. However, the law of 28 February 1967 limits this type of coverage to the Instituto Nacional de Previsión Social (INPS) and to insurance societies.

Workmen's compensation was incorporated into the social security system by a law of 14 November 1967, which thus absorbed the portfolios of private insurers then representing approximately 30% of their total premium income.

Since midyear in 1969 private companies have ceased new operations and the last policies subscribed with them expired in July, 1970. The payment of lump sums to victims or beneficiaries has been replaced by pensions in the new social security system.

Agents and Brokers. Insurance transactions are conducted by brokers and *prepostos* and, in a secondary way, by general agents. Legal rules, bylaws, and circulars from the Supervisory Office regulate the profession.

Public Insurance. Public insurance is organized through the Reinsurance Institute of Brazil (IRB), a body which has unusual impact on insurance policy and practice (see Section III). In some states of the Union, insurance is monopolized by entities whose social stock is majority owned by the government.

Reinsurance. No private market exists for reinsurance. Activities in this field belong to the Brazilian Reinsurance Institute, which receives the cessions of private institutions and establishes procedures and requirements for its development in the total market. Private companies normally act as retrocessionars from the Institute, although their risks may be placed in foreign markets when surpluses are not absorbed by this body or the national market.

II. FORM AND OPERATION OF PRIVATE INSURERS

Basic Legal Rules. These include the Code of Commerce of 25 June 1850, the Civil Code of 1 January 1916, the law-decree of 21 November 1966 which creates the Sistema Nacional de Seguros Privados (National Private Insurance System), the decree of 13 March 1967 which regulates the law-decree of 21 November 1966, and the law of 1 December 1970 concrening minimum stocks.

Judicial Nature. This is conducted through stock companies or cooperatives.

Social Purpose. This is limited exclusively to insurance activities.

Operations Area. A company may operate in all lines of insurance simultaneously provided minimum stock requirements are met. Reinsurance is monopolized by the Brazilian Reinsurance Institute; cooperatives may operate only in farm and health insurance. Foreign companies are forbidden to insure goods of government or of official bodies and institutions.

Minimum Capital Requirements. Both national and foreign companies are supervised periodically by the National Private Insurance Board. A resolution of this Board of 6 November 1971 establishes the actual minimum capital requirements. Companies were to apply for the approval of the General Assembly of insurance companies before 25 May 1972.

The sum of 6,000,000 cruzeiros (about $1,200,000) is required for companies in all lines of insurance, with 3,000,000 cruzeiros for companies operating only in life insurance, and 3,000,000 for those operating only in non-life lines.

For both Brazilian and foreign companies, the expended disbursed stock constitutes the warrant deposit (half of the subscribed stock). Ten percent of this must be paid when applying for authorization, and the remaining 40% before beginning operations. These disbursements must be invested in the type of goods considered proper for covering technical reserves.

Authorization Procedure. Each Brazilian company must produce a certificate of constitution as a commercial organization and an invoice of deposit for the disbursed social stock in the Bank of Brazil. Additional documentation required includes social statutes, technical bases, rates, policies, proposals and contracts to be operated.

In addition, a foreign company must produce a certificate stating that technical reserves will be used in Brazil only, the credentials of the person representing the company in Brazil, a certificate of its lawful operation in its homeland, and proof that reciprocity exists for Brazilian companies in the homeland.

The actual procedure for gaining authorization begins with an application addressed to the National Private Insurance Board. The Ministry of Industry and Commerce will issue a resolution after receiving a report from the Private Insurance Supervisory Office. The authorization carries a Royalty Card, which must be registered in the Supervisory Office and recorded in the Register of Commerce. It is then published in the "Official Journal" of the Union.

After publication, the insurance company must certify before the Supervisory Office that the shares corresponding to the Brazilian Reinsurance Institute have been subscribed within ninety days. Authorization is not final until a need for the company in the national insurance market has been demonstrated. If authorization is denied, appeal may be made before the president of Brazil.

Foreign companies have to follow the same procedure as Brazilian companies to gain authorization. Authorization will be withheld, however, if Brazilian companies are not authorized to operate in the foreign country.

Authorizations for both Brazilian and foreign insurance companies has been suspended for a three-year period by a resolution of the Ministry of Industry and Commerce as of 27 July 1970.

Reporting Obligations. Both Brazilian and foreign companies are required to publish the annual report, balance sheet, and profits and loss account in the Official Journal of the Union and in two other newspapers of wide circulation before 27 February each year. These also must be submitted to the Supervisory Office before 31 March annually. The company must also send the Supervisory Office a report of its general meetings, a list of agents and authorized representatives, any change in the administrative board, balance sheets, and other general reports. It is required to maintain the operations records established by the Supervisory Office. In addition it must send the Office statistical information on operations completed during each three-month period within forty-five days after the end of each period.

III. CONTRACTING

Basic Legal Rules. These include the law-decree of 21 November 1966, the decree of 13 March 1967, and the decree of 7 December 1967.

Policies. The market requires standard clauses and policies which have been prepared by technical commissions with aid from insurers, the Brazilian Reinsurance Institute, officers of the Supervisory Office, and even deputies of commerce and transportation activities. The National Private Insurance Board approves policies plus general and special conditions of required insurances. In other branches the Private Insurance Supervisory Office approves such documents.

Tariffs. All companies must submit their rates of minimum premiums and proposed reforms or new risks for approval from the Insurance Supervisory Office. Some rates have been ruled as obligatory, standard, and exclusive. Tariffs of obligatory insurances are established by the National Private Insurance Board.

Compulsory Insurances. Automobile insurance is required for all owners of motor vehicles as of October 1969. It is based on a system of objective civil responsibility in which compensation is paid on proof of damage, regardless of the driver's guilt. It provides 10,000 cruzeiros ($2,000) in case of death or permanent disability and 2,000 cruzeiros for associated medical service expenses; it may be reviewed by the National Private Insurance Board. Losses in excess of basic compensation may be recovered under tort liability.

Export Credit Insurance was established in 1965 and has been required since 1967 for exporting companies which use loans granted by public financial institutions. Its obligatory nature is conditioned by a statement made by the National Private Insurance Board according to a decree of 5 September 1969. It covers commercial, political, and extraordinary risks. No insurance policy for export credit may be issued unless the Brazilian Reinsurance Institute accepts its reinsurance. It is also authorized for retrocessions in foreign countries.

An obligatory insurance covering fire and transport of goods belonging legally to individuals was established in 1966 and bylawed in December 1967. Fire coverage is required for furnishings, installations and real estate in Brazil which separately or jointly has a value equal to or more than 20,000 cruzeiros ($4,000); transport coverage affects major risks inherent to national land, air, and sea transport of goods of value equal to or greater than 5,000 cruceiros.

In 1939 Brazil subscribed to the Warsaw Convention which regulates the required insurance for plane passengers and crew and the civil responsibility for damages to third parties. Minimum stocks for coverage were established later in the Ottawa Convention. The Brazilian Air Code makes this insurance obligatory, and its control is under the Civil Aeronautics Department.

Insurance covering the civil responsibility of highway transports was established in 1966 and has been required since 1969. The insurance grants the transport company payment of compensation owed to the owners of transported merchandise when losses are caused by accidents occurring during transportation. No limit exists for this compensation. The transporter is responsible unless he can prove that the loss was due to an accident or major outside force. All transport not made by highway—such as river, sea, lake, airway—still is not regulated. Fire insurance is also required for real estate under the law of horizontal property.

The following required insurances established by law decree of 21 November 1966 and regulated by decree of 7 December 1967, have not yet been enforced: (1) ship owners' civil responsibility insurance, (2) urban builders' civil responsibility for damages on persons or things insurance, (3) warrant insurance for performance of obligations of real estate builders and for payment of buyers, (4) insurance of goods given as a warrant of loans of financing for public financial institutions.

A special system has been established for the coverage of goods, rights, loans, and services of organizations of the public administration and societies partially subsidized or directly or indirectly controlled by them. These risks are distributed by an auction among the insuring companies, excluding foreign companies. The auction takes place in the Reinsurance Institute. Co-insurance among successful companies is required when the risk exceeds 100,000 cruceiros.

Goods, loans, and rights of some Brazilian states must be made with insurance companies when the majority of the shares belong to the state government.

The insurance of international transport of imported merchandise must be made in insuring companies established in Brazil except when the Brazilian government permits total or partial coverage in a foreign country. This resolution is not applied to insurances whose foreign subscription is regulated by conventions signed or approved by Brazilian authorities.

Foreign Insurance. Subscription of insurance or reinsurance in foreign countries is forbidden except when there is no comparable coverage inside

Brazil or it is inconvenient for national interests; the cession to foreign companies must be made by the Reinsurance Institute of Brazil. The contracting of insurance in foreign currency is also prohibited except in special cases mentioned by law (international transportation, ships' mortgages made in foreign currency outside Brazil, credit to exportation), and this is controlled by the Central Bank of Brazil according to rules of the Reinsurance Institute of Brazil.

IV. TECHNICAL RESERVES

Basic Legal Rules. These include the law of 31 December 1964 and the law-decree of 21 November 1966 creating the National Monetary Council, the 13 March 1967 decree, the Central Bank Resolution of 26 June 1968, and the resolution of the National Council of Private Insurance of 21 July 1971.

Classes. Mathematical (life) classes are integrated within the group called Non-Committed Technical Reserves. With respect to individual-life classes, these reserves must be determined quarterly by a value equivalent to committments related to enforced contracts, additional clauses, and capital increases in policies with shares in profits.

Non-amortized items of acquisition can be deducted from their amount (which must be amortized within five years by equal quotas in each fiscal year. This must also include at least the comprised commissions of the first year and costs for medical examinations.

Regarding contracts made within the twelve months before the reserve evaluation, no costs may be deducted higher than 50% of net premiums of the first year collected in this period and relative to enforced policies. A company may make a simplified quarterly calculation, previously fixed, by applying to the Superintendent, but this system does not replace the actual reserve calculation at the end of each fiscal year. In any event, apart from the system used, the value of the reserves can never be less than that corresponding to the technical notes approved by the Superintendent.

Regarding group life insurance, the reserve must be calculated monthly in accordance with the technical note approved by the Superintendent. However, a simplified method also is authorized, which consists of 20% of the premiums retained during the three months before the evaluation date.

All insurance reserves must be invested in Brazil. Before 31 December 1967 all reserves had to be invested in real estate and urban mortgages; loans on life policies; federal, state, or municipal treasury obligations; stock company shares and obligations quoted on the stock market; and deposits in savings banks and other banks (law-decree, 7 May 1940). Before 1967 investments in treasury obligations were quite reduced because they were not readjustable, in banking deposits due to inflation, and in company shares and obligations due to low quoting on the stock market. With the enforcement of the Central Bank Resolution of 26 June 1968, a new order was established whereby fundamental characteristics, among other aspects, included the necessity of investing a minimum of 50% in National Treasury Readjustable Obligations of annual reserve increase, corrected by the average increase index of the total market during the last two years.

The current investment situation is governed by the resolution of the National Council of Private Insurance of 21 July 1971, complemented by that of the National Monetary Council of 22 July 1971. These resolutions established a new regime, whose general characteristics are the following:

The so-called noncommitted technical reserves (Mathematics, Current Risks and Retrocession Guaranty Fund) must be invested in (1) readjustable obligations of the national Treasury, (2) bills of exchange of the national Treasury deposits in commercial or developmental banks or deposits in economic savings banks, (3) IRB shares, (4) shares, obligations or convertible obligations into shares of stock companies of open capital negotiable on the stock market, or in new shares, obligations or convertible obligations into shares issued by companies destined for use of basic industry, (5) new shares or nominal value increases of shares owned up to 31 December 1967, by means of discounts, subscription to capital increase, (6) participation in investment funds, (7) urban real estate, (8) loans with mortgage guaranty on urban real estate, (9) rights resulting from promissory contracts for urban real estate, (10) participation in financing operations, with monetary correction, undertaken by the National Bank of Economic Development, (11) participation in tourism approved by the Brazilian Tourism Company EMBRATUR.

In addition, the so-called committed technical reserves (pending claims) must be invested in (1) readjustable obligations of the national Treasury, (2) national Treasury Bills of Exchange, deposits in commercial or developmental banks, or deposits in savings banks, (3) shared obligations or convertible shares of stock companies with open capital, negotiable on the stock market, or in new shares, obligations, or convertible obligations into shares issued by companies for the use of basic industries.

Premium reserves are integrated in the group called noncommitted technical reserves and are called non-expired risk reserves; these are derived monthly by an amount equivalent to the following percentages: transport (25% of premiums retained in the preceding three months), internal credit (35% of premiums retained in the preceding twelve months), and remaining branches—insurance to be paid within a determined period (30% of premiums retained during the preceding twelve months), and insurance paid monthly (25% of premiums retained in three preceding months).

Outstanding losses are integrated into the group called committed technical reserves, which includes the following two types of reserves: (1) the so-called claims reserves to be liquidated, which are made up monthly by an amount equal to the indemnification pending payment for occurred claims, the recuperation through ceded reinsurance being deducted, and (2) the so-called expired insurance reserves, which must be constituted monthly by an amount equivalent to corresponding capital to be paid out upon expiration of contracts, deducting the reinsured part.

For deviations of loss ratio, there was the so-called contingency reserve which, by resolution of the National Council of Private Insurance of 21 July 1971, was cancelled at the end of that year.

Fluctuation of values is called security oscillation reserve and has to be constituted annually, being calculated by the difference between its joint recorded value and the value quoted on the stock market.

Two additional reserves are noted: (1) reserves with monetary correction, which are required for companies operating in insurance with monetary correction clauses, and (2) Retrocession Guaranty Fund, a reserve destined to respond in a subsidiary form to the IRB retrocession responsibilities, which must be constituted annually by an amount equivalent to 10% of the joint profit these retrocessions obtain for each company. This fund is considered as a noncommitted reserve.

General Requirements of Goods To Be Used as Reserve Covers. All goods fit for reserve coverage must be registered with the Superintendent of Insurance and may not be taxed or transferred without previous authorization. In case of this authorization, they should be substituted by other goods fit for reserve coverage; SUSEP can also authorize the releasing of goods guaranteeing the committed technical reserves for liquidation of claims included in these reserves.

Real estate, moreover, must be recorded in the General Register of real estate, and the value applied to guarantee the reserves may not be greater than the acquisition value, plus the accessory costs (transmissions, deed taxes, registration, and brokerage commissions) and monetary correction to the limit permitted by the application of coefficients fixed by the General Coordination and Planning Ministry.

Urban real estate cannot be comprised in the National Residence System.

Shares, obligations and convertible obligations in open capital company shares must have had an average quote no less than their nominal value during the past eighteen months.

Shares or securities of companies belonging to one shareholding group can be admitted up to their nominal value only, unless they are open capital companies authorized by the National Monetary Council.

Readjustable National Treasury Obligations may not be sold until two years after their purchase.

General Limits of Investment. The difference between noncommitted reserves calculated to the end of each quarter and those recorded in the balance to 31 December 1967 30% (individual-life) or 50% (remaining branches) should be invested in National Treasury Readjustable obligations.

Such percentages may be raised to 45% and 75% respectively, if considered advisable by the Superintendent of Insurance.

The remaining investment may be made in numbers (2) to (11) mentioned previously, up to 30% of the respective partial total or maximum limit for each of these investments or deposits, although numbers (7), (8), and (9) form a joint unit in this respect. Moreover, regarding numbers (4) and (5), there may not be a concentration higher than 5% of the total value of the security reserves of the same company by a figure higher than 10% of its respective capital.

Twenty-five percent of committed reserves must be invested in National Treasury readjustable obligations. Mortgage guaranty loans on urban real estate are fit for reserve coverage up to 80% of their value.

V. REINSURANCE

Basic Legal Rules. These include the law-decree of 21 November 1966 and the decree of 13 March 1967 (numbers 60.459 and 60.460).

Required Procedures. The only authorization is the Reinsurance Institute of Brazil (see VIII, Institutional Bodies), since its acceptances can be freely placed on the foreign market or retroceded in its own national market.

The acceptance of retrocessions by insuring companies of the country is required; nevertheless, they are not authorized to operate in retroceded branches or classes whose allotment shall be undertaken by the Institute in proportion to the volume of each company, except where general interests in the market advise another distribution formula.

Foreign reinsurance companies cannot operate directly in Brazil except in some insurance lines such as maritime and air hulls, in which cases cessions from national insurers may be received without meditation from the Institute when they are surplus and not placed in the country. Nevertheless, in such cases the application of premiums and technico-economic conditions similar to those offered by the Institute regarding its own retention for such business is required.

These companies, in accordance with the technical and commercial requirements of each case and with the general directions of the National Council of Private Insurance, are free to determine the type of reinsurance to be used and all conditions applicable for its execution. The action policy usually is based on the following principles: (1) reinsurance based on the excess of loss system, (2) application of minimum premiums, and (3) reciprocity with respect to retrocessions abroad.

To guarantee its retrocessions, the Institute maintains a reserve fund integrated by 10% of the profits resulting annually from such retrocessions to the national insurers themselves. Fifty percent of this sum may be kept provided no less than 6% interest is paid.

Retrocessions on foreign markets shall be undertaken through an international concurrence system (remembering the reciprocity system indicated above), where intervention is needed from a special commission for placing risks abroad. This is integrated by representatives of the Institute (which presides over it), the Ministry of Industry and Commerce, and an interested insurer and insuree.

VI. TAXES

Basic Legal Rules. These include the law of 20 October 1966, the Central Bank resolution of 28 October 1966, the Central Bank circular of 20 December 1966, the Insurance Superintendency circular of 11 March 1966, and the law-decree of 7 October 1969.

Taxes and Loading on Premiums. The tax rate on financial operations is equivalent to 1% on life insurance and personal accident insurance premiums and 2% on the premiums of other types of insurance. Since 1969 the following are exempt from these taxes: (1) operations in which the insured is affiliated directly or indirectly with a federal, state, or municipal body, (2) compulsory insurance subscribed by the National Bank of Habitation to the limit of 200 times the highest minimum salary enforced in the country, (3) export credit insurance, (4) international merchandise transport insurance, and (5) reinsurance operations.

Premiums for personal accident insurance, medical and hospitalization insurance, and some life insurance are deducted from gross income when calculating personal income taxes. Life and personal accident insurances are exempt from succession taxes.

All companies operating in obligatory civil responsibility insurance for automobiles must pay a special rate of 2% on the tariff premiums collected for maintaining an indemnification fund for traffic victims when the vehicle is unknown. This fund is administered by the IRB.

Taxes and Loadings over Profits. Insuring companies are subject to taxes common to service rendering companies.

VII. PRODUCTION (AGENTS)

Basic Legal Rules. These include the law of 29 December 1964, the law-decree of 21 November 1966, the decree of 13 March 1967, and the Private Insurance Superintendency circular of 12 July 1967.

Kinds of Agents. Brokers or free agents act as professional intermediaries, both as natural or legal individuals. General agents who cannot act as brokers are simple representatives of various insuring companies and are the legal substitutes of brokers when necessary.

Previous Requirements. Brokers have to be Brazilians or foreigners with permanent residency, be released from military service, have no criminal record, have no record of bankruptcy, and be professionally and technically trained for serving as brokers. This is achieved through serving for two or more years as a legal substitute of a broker, passing an examination, or through certification of professional exercise given by the corresponding trade union or the Superintendent.

The legal substitutes must be certified according to Brazilian laws; they must live in Brazil; their directors, managers, or administrators must fulfill the general requirements mentioned above.

Authorization. A certificate of authorization is granted by the Superintendent, which must be published in the official newspaper and recorded in the brokers' Trade Union Register. This authorization is granted if legal requirements are filled; if one is rejected, he may refer the decision to the Insurance Superintendent.

Bail. Bail must be furnished in cash or in public debt securities in an amount equivalent to the minimum monthly salary enforced where activities are to be conducted.

Agency Contracts. These do not exist in Brazil since the role of the agent is not typified and since brokers act independently with no contract between insuring companies.

Commissions. Brokers receive the following normal percentages, pre-established by rates: fire, 20%; personal accident, 30%; voluntary automobile, 10%; required automobile, 8%; transport, 15%. In the remaining branches commissions vary in relation to the insurance modality. In some branches, moreover, a 5% bonus exists on collected premiums to compensate for other services such as inspection of risks, etc. The basic compensation for general agents varies between 5% and 10%, according to the branch, plus 15% on the profit of the agency.

Official Protection. No official association exists although a corporative group does represent the Insurance Brokers Union and deals with problems and interests of the profession. Membership is not required.

Neither brokers nor their proxies may exercise public office or conduct activities in semi-state-owned companies. Neither can they be partners, administrators, proxies, or employees of insurance companies. The same holds true for partners and directors of legal brokerage companies.

No specific laws govern portfolio rights.

Insurance brokers are included in the national social security program since they are legally considered to be autonomous workers. A monthly percentage, determined from their commissions, is designated for this purpose and is paid by each insurer.

When no broker negotiates an insurance operation, the insurer may not discount commissions. In this event the quantity usually used for brokerage fees must be deposited by the insurance company in the Reinsurance Institute of Brazil, which will use the funds for paying general necessities of brokers (see training courses).

VIII. INSTITUTIONAL BODIES

Governmental Entities.   These include the following:

1. National Council of Private Insurance (CNSP), which is an independent organ of the Ministry of Commerce and Industry which supervises legislation on private insurance fulfillment and orients activities in the national insurance market. This is not an executive or technical organ but one of orientation and policy. Its agreements are of a generic nature and integrate insurance activities within the context of the country's economic policy. The Council is composed of the Ministers of Industry and Commerce, Treasury, Economic Planning and Coordination, Health, Work and Social Security, and Agriculture, as well as the Superintendent of Insurances, the president of the Reinsurance Institute of Brazil, a representative of the National Medicine Council, and three representatives of private enterprise designated by the President of the Republic.

2. Superintendent of Private Insurance (SUSEP), which is the delegated organ of the National Council of Private Insurance (CNSP) and carries out the functions of the organization regarding constitution, organization, performance of private insuring companies; it is a specialized technical group. It is a public-rights group with its own legal responsibilities, and administrative and financial autonomy. The Superintendent of Insurance is appointed by the president of the Republic, as proposed by the Minister of Industry and Commerce.

3. Reinsurance Institute of Brazil (IRB), which is a private rights group with legal responsibility and joint economy concerned with regulating co-insurance operations, reinsurance and retrocessions, and promotion of insurance activities in Brazil. Its capital stock is constituted by 15 million cruceiros ($3,000,000) and this may be raised to 35 million. Half of this sum belongs to the state (National Institute of Social Security), and the rest is subscribed by insurance companies authorized to operate in Brazil. It is administered by a council comprised of the president, vice-president, director of operations, and administrative and financial director, all of whom are designated by the president of the Republic as proposed by the Minister of Commerce and Industry. The Institute is assisted by a consulting, coordination, and advisory group, the Technical Council, and a Fiscal Council. The Technical Council issues reports on matters presented by the president of the Institute regarding (a) the fixing of regulating norms of co-insurance operations and those of reinsurance and retrocessions; (b) initiation of institutional operations in new insurance modalities and fixing the limits to be used in each one; (c) the fixing of norms for liquidation claims and the solving of controversies

between insurers and insurees or between these and the Institute itself; (d) regulation of the Retrocession Guaranty Fund; (e) establishment of norms on public auctions regarding distribution of insurance provided by official companies on the private insurance market.

Basic functions of the Fiscal Council include examining the official books and accounting documents, relaying information on quarterly reports or any other matter of economic or administrative interest to the president or Technical Council, and approving or disapproving reports on the balance and annual accounts of the Institute.

Technical service departments in the Institute include Operation in the Country, Loan Security, Operations Abroad and Special Insurance, Legal, Claims Liquidations, Financial, and Administrative.

4. National Monetary Council, which is a public group in charge of establishing regulations for investment policy of insurance companies' technical reserves. It establishes what investments are required and the criteria for determining security, liquidity, and profitability.

5. Consulting Commissions, which are integrated in the National Council of Private Insurance and advise and issue reports of a required nature. These include the Commissions of Health, Work, Transport, Housing, Rural, Aeronautics, Credit, and Brokers.

6. National Insurance College, which was established in July 1971. This school provides specialized training for insurance professions and functions as a foundation subsidized by the IRB, by the National Federation of Insurance Companies, and by the Insurance Superintendency.

Associations. These include the following:

1. National Federation of Private Insurance and Capitalization Companies (FENASEG), which is integrated by trade unions of private insurance and capitalization entities. It deals with questions regarding private insurance, from publicity to the defense and representation of their interests before the government and Parliament. Consequently, it participates in Consulting Commissions of the National Council of Private Insurance, in the special commissions of the Insurance Superintendency, and in the Permanent Commission or Technical Council of the Reinsurance Institute of Brazil.

2. National Insuring Entities Unions, which are private institutions integrated by insurance and capitalization companies, through which the Federation mentioned above is constituted. Activities of these unions are limited to a specified state. They exist in São Paulo, Guanabara, Río de Janeiro, Bahía, Minas Gerais, Paraná, Río Grande do Sul, and Pernambuco.

3. Land Insuring Federation, which is an organ of foreign insurance companies operating in Brazil.

4. Regional Unions of Insurance Brokers, which are private groups. Outstanding ones include the Pernambuco Brokers Union and those of Bahía, Minas Gerais, Guanabara, São Paulo, Paraná, and Río Grande do Sul.

5. International Association of Insurance Rights, which is a private association. A member of the international AIDA, it is made up of outstanding insurers, professors, and jurists to study and promote insurance law.

6. Other associative groups include the Brazilian Institute of Actuaries and the Brazilian Society of Insurance Sciences.

IX. CHARACTERISTICS OF THE SIXTIES

Export Credit Insurance. Export credit insurance was regulated for the first time in 1962 when it was authorized by an association comprised of the Ministry of the Treasury (through the National Bank of Economic Desarrollo), the IRB, and private insurance companies who wanted this regulation and were responsible for covering commercial risks. Through a law of June 1965 and a decree-regulation of November 1965 commercial risks were to be covered exclusively by private insurers. The government is responsible for covering political and extraordinary risks through the IRB. (See Contracting)

Insurance on Goods of Public Entities. The first regulation was published in 1962 to cover risks of groups of an official or semistate nature. Such insurance was to be contracted in companies operating in Brazil to take maximum advantage of the national market. Surplus was placed in the IRB or abroad through the Institute. Life insurance, workmen's compensation, and agricultural risks insurance are excluded from this regulation and are treated separately. In October 1966 it was established that insurance for goods, rights, credits, and services of centralized associations of the Union, Autorquias (half private—half state-owned self governing bodies), was to be negotiated through public auction among national insurance companies. The auction was to be undertaken by the IRB; no brokers or administrators were allowed in such insurance, and coinsurance was required for capital over 100,000 cruceiros.

Regulation of the Insurance Brokerage Profession. The law of 29 December 1964 began the true institutionalization of insurance brokers' activities. This law and later complementary laws regulate the professional rights and duties of brokers, establish a procedure for avoiding illegal competition, and fix norms for their designation, nomination and official register, both in general branches and in life insurance and capitalization insurance companies.

Collections through Banks. The 8 September 1966 decree, which establishes a new procedure for collecting premiums through national banking institutions, provides for the reduction of internal costs of private institutions and aids in collecting receipts.

Establishment of the National Private Insurance System. By law-decree of 21 November 1966 the national system of private insurance was established, which places Brazil among the first countries worldwide to have an organic group of regulating up-do-date legal norms for insuring institutions. The most outstanding aspects of this new system include (1) specification of state and private organs and entities which comprise the system, (2) establishment of a series of required insurances leading to the strengthening of the national insurance market and the protection of the country's economy, and (3) conditioning of the technical reserves investments to the directions of the National Monetary Council so that the criteria for profitability, security, and liquidity are always used.

Socialization of Workmen's Compensation Insurance. Work accident insurance was provided by stock companies (90% of the market) and cooperative companies which also specialized in coverage of agricultural risks. In September 1967 this branch was placed under the National Institute of Social Security which is responsible for providing indemnifications.

Required Civil Responsibility for Automobiles. The introduction of required insurance, including "civil responsibility of owners of automobile vehicles of land routes," was undertaken by a law-decree of 21 November 1966. This is regulated by the National System of Private Insurance. A decree of 7 December 1967 stated that obligatory coverage would begin on 1 October 1969 regarding civil automobile responsibility only. The National Council of Private Insurance established uniform norms for applicable premiums and certificate models to be used. (See compulsory insurances).

Strengthening of the National Insurance Market. Governmental policy in this area is reflected by the 24 July 1970 law-decree (put into effect by the 27 October 1970 decree) granting advantages to the merger and incorporation of insurance companies and by the 1 December 1970 law, whose outstanding aspects include the following: (1) Adoption of a criteria for fixing minimum capital for companies for each branch in the regions set up for insurance operations in the country. (2) Establishment of a responsibility regime regarding fiscal administrators and counselors of insurance companies beginning required liquidation processes guaranteed by the unavailability of their goods. (3) Self-limitation of state activities through prohibition of authorization for the functioning of new companies with direct or indirect participation of their capital in federal, state, or municipal public powers.

New Forms on the Constitution of Technical Reserves. Although this does not chronologically come within the sixties, its importance demands incorporation in this appendix. The norms compiled in the May 1971 resolution of the National Council of Private Insurance and developed by the resolution of the National Monetary Council and the circular of the Insurance Superintendent, jointly comprise a systematic plan for the classification, constitution, investment, and accounting of technical reserves. It also contains the necessary transitory dispositions for gradual application of the new system.

X. FUNDAMENTAL LEGISLATION

Chronological Order

29 December 1964—Law regulating the insurance brokerage profession (No. 4.594)

31 December 1964—Law creating the National Monetary Council (No. 4.595)

16 June 1965—Law regulating Export Credit Insurance (No. 4.678)

23 September 1965—Decree ruling on the Insurance Brokerage regime (No. 56.900)

18 November 1965—Decree ruling on Export Credit Insurance (No. 57.286)

20 October 1966—Law instituting the tax on financial operations (No. 5.143)

28 October 1966—Central Bank resolution ruling on tax on financial operations (No. 40)

21 November 1966—Law-decree establishing the National Private Insurance System (No. 73)

13 March 1967—Decree ruling on law-decree establishing the National Private Insurance System (No. 60.459)

13 March 1967—Decree reforming the statutes of the Brazilian Reinsurance Institute (IRB) (No. 60.460)

23 October 1967—Decree establishing new norms on minimum capital and initiation of operations (No. 61.589)

7 December 1967—Decree ruling on obligatory insurances (No. 61.867)

26 June 1968—Central Bank resolution on technical reserve applications (No. 92)

5 August 1968—Private Insurance Superintendency Resolution on technical reserves constitution (No. 30)

4 September 1969—Law-decree regulating automobile insurance (No. 814)

1 December 1970—Law on minimum capital (No. 5.627)

21 July 1971—National Council of Private Insurance Resolution on constitution of reserves (No. 5)

By Subject

General Dispositions—(1) Law-decree establishing the National Private Insurance System, 21 November 1966; (2) decree ruling on the above law-decree, 13 March 1967; (3) decree reforming the statutes of the Brazilian Reinsurance Institute (IRB), 13 May 1967; (4) decree establishing new norms on capital and initiation of operations, 23 October 1967; (5) law on minimum capital, 1 December 1970.

Taxes—(1) law instituting the tax on financial operations, 20 October 1966; (2) Central Bank resolution ruling on the tax on financial operations 28 October 1966.

Brokerage—(1) Law ruling on the insurance brokerage profession, 29 December 1964; (2) Central Bank resolution ruling on the insurance brokerage regime, 23 September 1965.

Technical Reserves—(1) Central Bank resolution, 26 June 1968; (2) Private Insurance Superintendency resolution, 5 August 1968; (3) National Private Insurance Council resolution, 21 July 1971.

Required Insurance—decree of 7 December 1967.

Automobile Civil Responsibility—law-decree regulating the automobile civil responsibility insurance, 4 September 1969.

Export Credit—(1) Law regulating coverage, 16 June 1965; (2) decree regulating export credit insurance, 18 November 1965.

Chile

I. GENERAL INFORMATION

Historical Note. Authorization to begin insurance activities was granted to La Chilena, today known as La Chilena Consolidada, in 1853. This is the oldest Latin American insurance company. The Civil and Commercial Codes enacted in the decade between 1857 and 1858 were the first rules to regulate the insurance contract. The law of December 1927 governing nationalization of insurance commerce forbids the establishment of foreign companies, creates the Insurance Supervisory Office, and establishes the Reinsurance Fund of Chile. Law-decree 251 of 20 May 1931, still in force, established the legal system for insurance companies, corporations, stock exchanges, and the Insurance Supervisory Office. The Government Insurance Institute was created in 1953.

Official Control. Official control comes through the Insurance Supervisory Office, insurance companies, stock companies, and the stock exchange. The Supervisory Office also acts as arbitrator among insurers, intermediaries, and insured persons.

Professional Statute. The primary representative of professional insurers is the Association of Insurers of Chile, which is comprised of the companies that operate in different activities; the Life Insurers Association, which includes different companies operating in this branch; the Professional Unions of Insurance Producers, classified by life and other branches, which represent their associates' interests before public and insurer authorities; and the Association of Claims Adjusters, an organization of professionals in charge of damage survey.

Market Structure. This is formed by 144 national companies which hold 84.5% of the total premiums of the market. The remainder are foreign companies. There are 170 companies in all.

International Expansion. At present there is practically no international expansion.

Workmen's Compensation. This is provided through the Social Insurance Service, the National Health Service, Provision Funds, and Employers Mutual Society. A law of 1 February 1968 bans private companies from dealing in workmen's compensation or occupational hazards insurance.

Agents and Brokers. Except for general agents ("captives"), professional agents and commissioned agents are "free." Most work under labor-type contracts. Their legal status is well protected.

Public Insurance. Most public insurance is provided through the Institute of State Insurance, which provides life insurance required for private employees and required by institutions and official organizations.

Reinsurance. There is virtually no professional reinsurance since the Reinsurance Fund of Chile operates exclusively in this field. This institution accepts reinsurance not covered by the private sector, retaining for its own accounts amounts considered convenient and retroceding the excess in the domestic market or abroad.

II. FORM AND OPERATION OF PRIVATE INSURERS

Basic Legal Rules. These include the Commerce Code of 23 November 1865; the decree with force of law of 20 May 1931 concerning insurance companies, stock companies, and stock exchanges; and the law of 1 July 1970 which modifies the above-mentioned decree.

Legal Nature. This is provided through a stock company, mutual or cooperative society, the same as other groups authorized by law.

Social Purpose. These must be restricted exclusively to insurance and reinsurance operations.

Area of Operation. Permission to operate in the insurance market is limited to life and nonlife risks; simultaneous operation in both is forbidden.

Minimum Capital Requirements. Minimum capital required for national companies is 100 sueldos per year ($50,000).(SUELDO: Annual salary paid out in monthly increments.) The capital must be totally subscribed and disbursed. The president of the Republic, following a report from the Supervisory Office, can permit a smaller capital when the company is planning to insure risks not requiring so much capital. At least two-thirds of the capital must be subscribed and preserved by Chilean or foreign stockholders domiciled in Chile.

A minimum capital is not required for foreign companies, but the amount of capital must be reported to the Supervisory Office before permission to operate is granted. The constitution of foreign companies has not been allowed since 1927.

A guaranty deposit is not required although foreign companies must have invested a minimum of 1,000,000 escudos ($40,000) in Chile. They may invest 500,000 plus technical reserves if they operate only in marine insurance.

Process of Authorization. Documentation for national companies includes the constitution contract, social statutes, tariffs and policies, underwriting subscription certification, and disbursement of social capital.

In addition to the above, foreign companies must have authorized registration in their own country, must designate the person who is the representative in Chile, file a report of disbursement made by stockholders in Chile, file a report of disbursement made by stockholders to complete their social capital, and provide an authorized copy of the last balance sheet and a subsistence certificate of the society. In addition the society has to submit a report stating that it knows Chilean legislation, that it adheres to Chilean laws, especially in fulfilling Chilean obligations, and that the society has set up a special fund with marketable values in Chile to face such liabilities (this fund will be determined by the Supervisory Office according to the nature of each society.)

The procedure set forth for both national and foreign companies involves submitting a report to the Superintendent of Insurance Companies, stock companies, and commerce exchanges. After approval the report takes the form of a resolution which must be certified by the Treasury Ministry. The resolution will be published in the "Official Newspaper" and registered in the public Registration of the Supervisory Office and in the Commerce Registration. Approval is mandatory if all legal requisites are met. For permission to be denied there must be a cause. A denial cannot be appealed.

Reporting Obligations. For both national and foreign companies the director's report, balance sheet, and underwriting results account have to be submitted to the Supervisory Office within ninety days after the closing of each accounting period. In addition a report entitled "Superintendent's File," which contains information on investments, summary of each assets and liabilities account, list of stockholders, reinsurance movements, detailed production by branches, commissions or other remuneration paid to each agent of each branch, the number of issued policies, and details of administration expenses must be submitted.

Balance sheet and accounts and investment inventory must be published in a company record newspaper ten days before the date when the General Meeting takes place. Companies must maintain in public view a shareholders list with up-to-date information on the number of shares and corresponding addresses.

III. CONTRACTING

Basic Legal Rules. These are provided through the Commerce Code of 23 November 1865; the decree of 20 May 1931 on insurance companies, stock companies, and stock exchanges; and the Law of 1 July 1970 that modifies the above decree.

Policies. Policies must be authorized and approved by the Superintendency. This body may change policy forms in use without making these forms obligatory.

Tariffs. The Supervisory Office must approve tariffs. When advisable, they may annul tariffs in use and make other ones obligatory. Uniform tariffs exist for all companies. For special risks or for those whose insured capital is more than 1,000 minimum annual salaries ($500,000) it is possible to request a special premium rate from the Supervisory Office through the Tariff Committee of the Insurer Association. If approved, this becomes the tariff premium rate for a specific risk and is required for all companies in the market. In the case of hull risks, tariffs are fixed according to the reinsurance policies given to the Reinsurance Fund by the external market. The Supervisory Office fixes and regulates the interest and credit terms that companies can give their clients for the payment of premiums.

Required Insurance.   Compulsory insurances include the following:

1. Passenger and Pedestrian Accident Insurance of the Collective Transportation. This insurance provides indemnity payment to passenger or pedestrian in cases that produce (a) death (up to 10,000 escudos or $400. It can increase to twice this amount according to the victim's family obligations), (b) total or partial permanent incapacity (same provision as in the case of death), (c) temporary disability (up to one-thirtieth of the monthly salary—320 escudos daily or $12). This insurance also provides payment of hospitalization and pharmacy expenses, and medical bills when not covered by Social Provision Institutions. The premium of this insurance is included in the ticket price and is equivalent to 1% of the value. This monopolistic coverage is provided by the Insurance Institute of the Government.

2. Automobile Third Party Insurance. Established by law of July 1970, its coverage will be offered by the Government Insurance Institute and by private companies. It is based on a system of civil responsibility for bodily injury and material damages.

3. Exports Credit Insurance. Although this insurance is not yet in effect pending legal regulations, it is foreseen that commercial risks will be covered through the Export Credit Insurance Company and that political and catastrophic risks will be covered by the Bank of the Government of Chile. The Bank will handle the premiums and loss payments.

4. Compulsory Life Insurance for Private Employees. This must be contracted through the Insurance Institute of the Government.

5. Public Institutions Insurance. The following individuals and groups are required to be insured exclusively through the Insurance Institute of the Government: insurable risks which have their origin in acts or contracts performed by Social Prevision Funds; semipublic institutions, public enterprises or enterprises with an autonomous government administration; in general, all persons in positions created by law in which the government has representation or capital investment.

6. Other Insurances. The Reinsurance Fund of Chile covers all risks when no other company in the country can or will cover it or when the general interest of the national commerce insurance advises. However, the Supervisory Office must first grant authorization. The Reinsurance Fund will accept such risks in agreement with its Board of Directors.

Restrictions on Foreign Insurance.   Citizens or recognized organizations which wish to insure their goods established in Chile or any interests in companies not established in Chile shall pay a tax of 60% of the cost of the particular premium in Chile. The tax is not required when the insurance is executed abroad if no Chilean company will accept the risk. When an individual purchases life insurance abroad, he pays a tax equivalent to 60% of the annual premium to be paid abroad unless the insurance has been authorized by the Supervisory Office. All insurance purchased abroad requires prior permission of the Insurance Supervisory Office.

IV. TECHNICAL RESERVES

Basic Legal Rules.   These include the law-decree of 20 May 1931 regarding insurance companies, stock companies, and stock exchanges; and the law of 1 July 1970 modifying the law-decree.

Classes.   The constitution of mathematical (life) insurance is determined according to rules authorized by the Supervisory Office. The constitution of unearned premium reserve is determined according to procedures proposed by the Supervisory Office. It is usually about 40% of the retained premiums. No special system exists covering outstanding loss reserves.

Aside from the legal reserve (which consists of a general fund whose value equals at least half the social capital of the companies with a quota between 10% and 40% of its annual net profits), reserve funds also exist which have to do with the revaluation of capital itself, with the fluctuation of values, and with future dividends, all of which are regulated by tax laws.

With some exceptions, all reserves must be invested in Chile. These exceptions refer to agencies of foreign companies, legal investments of 1,000,000 and 500,000 escudos outside Chile, and mathematical reserves in life-group up to a maximum of 40% of their reserves. In the remaining instances, the general rules of investment are the following: up to a maximum of 60% in real estate; up to a maximum of 75% in stocks of national banks or stock companies; a minimum of 20% in goods of easy liquidation. There is no limit on investment in public debt, Chilean government bonds and mortgage banks, mortgage bonds of enterprises of public profit, first order engagements, deposits, credits and values of readjustable furnishings, real estate, cash deposits, time deposits in national banks, and mortgage guaranteed loans on urban real estate of income.

There are other compulsory investments, such as the purchase of shares in the Reinsurance Fund of the Educational Institutions Building Society, etc. This amount is determined by the Supervisory Office according to the capital and the company's reserve and the profit of each transaction.

General Requirements of Goods To Be Used as Reserve Covers.   In general all investments require prior permission of the Insurance Supervisory Office regarding its class and amount.

General Limits of Investment. As indicated in the above discussion of investment regarding foreign societies operating in life-group, the Supervisory Office can permit mathematical reserves of policies contracted in foreign currency to be invested in foreign values abroad to a maximum of 40% of total reserves.

V. REINSURANCE

Basic Legal Rules. These include decree with force of law of 20 May 1931 regarding insurance companies, stock companies, and stock exchanges; and law of 1 July 1970 which modifies the decree.

General Characteristics. All companies authorized to deal in direct insurance also are able to operate in reinsurance. Companies that operate in reinsurance only cannot be organized in the country with the exception of the Reinsurance Fund of Chile.

Each company, including the Government Insurance Institute, establishes its own limits of net retention on each kind of insurance, except for fire insurance. In this case maximum and minimum limits are fixed by the Supervisory Office. The excess retention may be placed with other national or foreign insurance groups through reinsurance agreements, although monies placed with foreign groups are exceptional and require permission through the Reinsurance Fund.

Private companies may accept direct foreign reinsurance without intervention of the Reinsurance Fund.

The primary function of the Reinsurance Fund of Chile is to accept the excess not covered by the private market (independent companies or their representatives). The Fund retains the amount determined to be convenient retroceding the excess to the national or foreign market. The first reinsurance surplus that the Fund receives from foreign companies should be offered to Chilean companies under conditions prescribed by its Board. Commissions drawn from these operations will be determined every six months by the Board of the Fund in accordance with the Supervisory Office.

The Reinsurance Union is a pool of fire insurers which absorbs the excess from dependent companies and retrocedes to all of them (without retaining any risk) in proportion to their respective cessions for the preceding fiscal year.

VI. TAXES

Basic Legal Rules. These include the decree with force of law of 20 May 1931 regarding insurance companies, stock companies, and stock exchanges, and the law of 1 July 1970 modifying the above decree.

Taxes and Loadings over Premiums. The fiscal profits tax is 4% of the net premiums of Chilean operations (6% for foreign companies). Life insurance is an exception with a tax of 10% of the first annual premium (15% for foreign companies). Mutual societies are exempt from this tax.

Other charges include the following: (1) Companies operating in fire insurance pay 2% of their net premiums to the maintenance of national firemen services; (2) Risks insured by companies not settled in Chile pay a tax of 60% of the premiums that would have been paid in Chile unless authorized otherwise by the Supervisory Office; (3) a tax of 1% of the net premiums retained by each company for reinsurance goes for upkeep of the Supervisory Office unless this deduction is placed abroad.

Taxes and Loading over Profits. The income tax is governed by Law 15.564, published in the official newspaper of the Chilean republic 14 January 1964. This tax is levied on incomes, capital gains, and any other profit causing an increase in net worth. It is applied to stock companies with a premium rate of 35%. The rate for capital gains is 20%. Dividends paid to shareholders by stock companies are not subject to any other tax except the personal income tax which Chilean citizens must pay. Its rate is progressive, going from 10% to 60%.

A housing pool tax is levied on the same incomes and profits which are subject to income tax (except for capital gains). The 5% rate will become 7% if instead of paying the tax the company chooses alternatives offered by the housing law.

A patrimonial tax, set up by law 17.073, modified by law 17.416 and published in the official journal of the Republic of Chile on 31 December 1968, is applied annually as a tax on net worth, or the difference between actual assets and expected liabilities noted in the annual balance. The rate is 0.5%.

The tax on sales and services, law 12.120, published in the official journal of the Republic of Chile on 30 October 1956, provides "cascade" taxing, that is, taxing on each sales transaction of movable property, and income from business and such services as commissions, interests, insurance premiums, rental income, etc. The rate on sales is 8% and on services is 17%. The rate is 18% for most insurance premiums. Insurances covering maritime and aerial transport of import and export merchandise, earthquake, and ship hull risk are exempt.

VII. PRODUCTION (AGENTS)

Basic Legal Rules. These include the law of 21 November 1944 declaring professional agents to be private employees; the law of 16 August and the decree of 20 December 1967 establishing the regulation of insurance producers, and the law of 1 July 1970 modifying the law-decree of 20 May 1931 regulating insurance companies.

Kinds of Agents. Once a year agents are classified according to the following groups: (1) Professional agents who are Chilean citizens who contract insurance and receive at least 60% of their annual income from this activity. If they operate in different branches of insurance they should receive in commissions at least $500 a year from policies sold to thirty-six different persons. If they sell life insurance, their commissions should equal at least one minimum annual salary derived from policies on fifteen different persons. (2) Commission agents are authorized citizens who do not meet the above mentioned requirements for professional agents. (3) General agents are insurance producers who have been given special responsibilities by the insurance company or by various insurance companies under the same administration. They may have several functions if authorized by the Superintendency.

Previous Requirements. Agents must be Chilean or foreigners living in Chile, over eighteen years of age, have a clean background, have the title of Commercial Agent and Traveler, be fit in all ways, pass the ability and knowledge examination to be taken at the Superintendency. These prerequisites must also be fulfilled by individual representatives—managers, and directors—anyone authorized to work in insurance production. In addition general agents must be classified as professional agents, must be certified, and must represent only one company.

Authorization. Authorization is granted by the Superintendency and must be recorded in the National Register for Travelers. Authorization may be granted to operate for one or more companies for most types of insurance, but for only one life insurance company. In fact, currently this authorization is not being given.

Surety. The agent must provide a guarantee for the insurance company for which he has been authorized and for the Superintendency. This guarantee may be in money, bonds, shares, deposit, or other guarantees, all determined by the Superintendency. The initial minimum guarantee must be for at least one monthly minimum salary for agents selling life insurance and at least two minimum salaries for other branches. These guarantees are reevaluated annually. For life insurance agents they are fixed by the Superintendency according to the volume and nature of operations conducted by the agent. For other branches the guarantee is 30% of the gross premiums sold through the agent in the preceding fiscal year.

Agency Contracts. Contracts for professional and general agents are similar to those of labor since agents are considered as private employees of the insurance company. Therefore, these contracts adhere to the work code and must be recorded in writing with date and resolution number specifying the individual as a professional insurance agent. This contract must be subscribed with each company for which the agent works. Every agent can be listed and, despite his classification, can work with as many companies as he and the companies agree on. Therefore all are legally free agents; no one is a captive agent except in the case of general agents.

Commissions. The regulations controlling commissions are made up of the following concepts: (1) The maximum commission for most branches of insurance is fixed by the Regulation on Insurance Producers, e.g., individual accidents, 21%; ordinary fire, 14%; hulls, 5.3%; robbery, 21%; civil responsibility, 16%; automobiles, 10.5%. If not expressly regulated, the commission cannot be higher than one-third of that of the reinsurance paid by the Reinsurance Fund of Chile unless authorized by the Superintendency. (2) Production bonuses, used solely for fire insurance, are applied on their additional coverages; their value may not exceed 8% of premiums of coverages subject to this regulation. (3) Professional and commission agents may be assigned special commissions by the insuring company provided the agent has been in the business for at least five years. Only additional coverage in fire insurance is affected and its maximum value is 1.5%. Special commission assignments are required for general agents in most branches, and the value is fixed annually by the Superintendency.

Official Protection.   An association which represents professional unions of insurance producers before government authorities, insurance authorities, and insurance companies discourages clandestine operations of the profession and illicit competition, and encourages professional groups of producers.

The following are causes of unfitness or incompatibility: to be employed by insurance companies, by the Reinsurance Fund of Chile, the Insurers Association of Chile, the Association of Life Insurers, the Union of Insurance Producers, or of legal persons who produce insurance; to be a manager, director, proxy, production chief, or representative of insurance companies or authorized persons producing insurance; to be manager, director, or employee of banking institutions, of credit, mortgage, or savings and loan institutions; to be a liquidator, a damage surveyor, or expert designated by the Superintendency, or to carry out activities which, in the opinion of the Superintendency, permit putting pressure on people to take out insurance or to buy it with a particular insurance company.

In the event an individual wants to increase his insurance or take out a new policy on the same risk, the policy should be set up as it was by the producer who provided the original insurance. Providing there is no declaration against the insurer, the original insurance shall remain in force, and the producer shall continue with the same insurance company.

In most branches of insurance, when an agent leaves an insurance company, he has the right to continue to receive remunerations due him from operations executed by him while he was with that company. This benefit ceases when the agent retires. The same holds true for producers of life insurance, but they will continue to receive permanent-type commissions two years after their retirement or after being transferred to another company.

Professional agents, as private employees of insurance companies, are included in the Social Security system. Companies pay their fees directly to the Prevision Fund. When agents work for different companies, all of them contribute toward the total fee.

VIII. INSTITUTIONAL BODIES

Governmental Entities. Insurance companies, stock companies, and the Stock Exchanges Supervisory Office are responsible to the Treasury Ministry which usually supervises the fulfillment of legislation on private insurance. These groups authorize the existence of insuring entities and approve their laws and amendments, financial operations, determine maximum retention limits for each company in fire and deposit or guarantee insurance once a year, approve premium tariffs and policy forms; fix minimum capital held by new stock companies, verify current risk reserves and mathematics of companies in accordance with the Superintendency, and authorize and fix the number and jurisdiction of branches, agents, and brokers of companies, as well as their commissions.

In addition, these organizations act as arbitrator without further appeal in litigations between insurance companies and between the companies and their agents or insurees.

The Reinsurance Fund of Chile is a joint economy institute which supervises reinsurance coverage of companies operating in Chile under legally established conditions. Its capital stock is represented by so-called class A shares (of the State), class B (of private companies), and class C (of the public in general) with a nominal unit value of 500 escudos. Companies are required to invest 5% of their capital and reserves in class B shares; the disbursed capital of the Fund is more than 2,000,000 escudos, of which 95% comes from contributions from private companies.

The directive council of the Fund is made up of seven persons: three designated by the president of the Republic and three by insurance companies, and the General Manager of the Fund, who is appointed by the president after being selected by five or more members of the directory.

The State Insurance Institute is a public group responsible to the Treasury Ministry and responsible for coverage of risks to authorized persons where the state has representation or owns capital stock. The Institute is also responsible for coverage of the compulsory accident insurance for passengers and pedestrians of collective locomotion.

The National Company of Export Credit Insurance is a joint economy group belonging to the State Insurance Institute and the national insurances companies. It is responsible for coverage of commercial risks derived from export credit; in addition it acts as an intermediary for placing political and extraordinary risks through the State Bank of Chile.

Associations. Insurers' associations include the following:

1. Insurers Association of Chile, which is comprised of companies operating in several branches. It develops labor union activities and proposes and finances premium tariffs applicable to insurees and insurers, subject to approval by the Superintendency. Insurers' associations must be approved by the president of the Republic after receiving a report from the Superintendency.

2. Associations of Life Insurers, which are groups of companies operating in life insurance. Activities of these groups are similar to those for Insurers Associations, but these pertain particularly to life insurance.

3. Reinsurance Union, which is a pool formed by almost all companies dealing in fire insurance.

4. Professional Unions of Insurance Producers, which collectively represent insurance professions with regard to public authorities, branch authorities, and insurance companies. They promote professional prestige and attempt to inhibit clandestine, illicit, or disloyal competition. These groups function in life and other branches of insurance.

5. Claims Adjusters Association is an organization which groups almost all who are professionally involved in revision and technical assessment of damages and disasters, whether they work independently or with an insurance company.

IX. CHARACTERISTICS OF THE SIXTIES

Insurance Cooperatives Regulation. On 23 February 1963 the Organic Cooperatives Law was published, thus making these cooperatives legal, although scarcely regulating them. Since then Law 17.318 of 1 August 1970 and other laws have affected these groups, allowing them a similar but preferential status to that of insurance companies.

Tariff Revision. In 1966 the Insurers Association of Chile and the Insurance Superintendence restructured the fire branch tariff, primarily lowering the tariff, providing for better insuring, and extending insurance to more individuals. A later study, still unfinished, was initiated into tariffs covering automobiles and marine transport.

Regulation of Insurance Producers. In 1967 the Regulation of Insurance Producers was approved, and the responsibility for its compliance rests with the Insurance Superintendency. This regulation established the status of insurance producers, fixed norms to be applied in insurance contracting, payment, and other aspects of administrative activities in insurance companies.

Compulsory Insurance for Public Transportation Passengers. This form of insurance was provided beginning in 1967, but only through the State Institute of Insurance.

Compulsory Insurance for Work Accidents and Professional Illnesses. The law of 1 February 1968 established this compulsory insurance for occupational accidents and illnesses through the Social Security Service, the Social Security Loan Banks, the National Health Service, and the Employer's Mutuals.

Exports Credit. In 1968 the administrative procedure for providing export credit insurance was established, but to date it has not gone into effect since regulations governing it have not been issued. Financing is to be provided through the National Company of Export Credit Insurance with capital contributed by private companies and the State Insurance Institute, which will cover commercial risks. Political and surplus commercial risks are covered by the State Bank of Chile.

Compulsory Civil Responsibility Insurance. Law 17.308 of 1 July 1970 establishes compulsory civil responsibility insurance for owners and drivers of motor vehicles. Financing is through the State Insurance Institute and private companies. Based on objective responsibility, this insurance covers damages to persons and things. It is not yet in effect as regulations governing it have not been issued.

Current Legislation Modifications. Law 17.308 of 1 July 1970 substantially modified the Commerce Code regarding regulation of stock companies, particularly in regard to formation and functioning of directories; it also changed the special legislation of insurance companies, giving greater power to the Insurance Superintendency which directly affected the administrative and financial progress of the institutions under its control.

X. FUNDAMENTAL LEGISLATION

Chronological Order

20 May 1931—Law-decree on insurance companies, stock companies, and stock exchanges (No. 251).

21 November1944—Law declaring professional insurance agents to be private employees.

5 April 1967—Law-decree regulating exports credit insurance (No. 3).

21 July 1967—Decree regulating export credit insurance (No. 3).

21 July 1967—Decree regulating accident insurance for passengers and pedestrians of public transportation (No. 1.130).

1 December 1967—Decree establishing the reconstructed text on the National Register of Traveling Salesmen.

20 December 1967—Decree approving regulation on insurance producers (No. 2.098).

1 February 1968—Law establishing compulsory insurance for work accidents and professional illnesses.

1 July 1970—Law (text modifying the decree—with force of law No. 251, on insurance companies, stock companies, and stock exchanges). (No. 17.308).

1 July 1970—Law establishing compulsory automobile civil responsibility insurance.

Classified Index

General Dispositions—(1) Decree with force of law on insurance companies, stock companies, and stock exchanges, 20 May 1931; (2) Law (text modifying the decree with force of law on insurance companies, stock companies, and stock exchanges), 1 July 1970.

Exports Credit Insurance—decree regulating this insurance, 5 April 1967.

Accident Insurance for Passengers and Pedestrians of Public Transportation—Law regulating this insurance, 21 July 1967.

Workmen's Compensation and Professional Illnesses—Law regulating this insurance, 1 February 1968.

Compulsory Automobile Civil Responsibility Insurance—law regulating this insurance, 1 July 1970.

Insurance Production—(1) Decree approving regulation on insurance production, 20 July 1967; (2) Law declaring professional insurance agents to be private employees, 21 November 1944; (3) decree establishing the reconstructed text on national salesman register, 1 December 1967.

Colombia

I. GENERAL INFORMATION

Historical Note. Law 57 of 1887 enforced the Terrestrial Code of Commerce, which included the first regulation of insurance activities. This law was annulled in 1971 by Decree 410 which established a new business code. The first insurance company, la Compañía Colombiana de Seguros, was established in 1874. Law 68 of 1924 established the first government control of insurances; this was completed in November 1927 by Law 105, Regulator of Insurance Companies, and in 1940 by Law-Decree 1.043. The Bank Supervisory Office began activities in 1927.

Official Control. Control is through the Bank Supervisory Office, which is under the Presidency of the republic. Its responsibilities cover both the formation and liquidation of insurance companies and their operations, including approval of policies, premiums, tariffs, balance sheet examinations, profit and loss accounts, reinsurance policy, etc.

Professional Statute. All professional portions of an insurance company are integrated into important associations such as asociaciones de Compañías de Seguros (ASECOLDA), of agents (ACODASE), of actuaries, of brokers and lawyers (Insurance Law Association). These organizations represent virtually all parts of professional insurance activities and they maintain links with official insurance bodies.

Market Structure. The Colombian insurance market is comprised of sixty-eight companies, fifty of which are national companies, collecting 90% of the income of the market. Foreign companies conduct 10% of the insurance activities. In the life insurance branch, the three most important companies collect about 60% of the total income of the market, thus reflecting a high degree of concentration. In other branches where concentration is also high, the rate is approximately 41%. The most important types of insurance are life (group and individual) with approximately 30% of the income of the various types, fire with 20%, and automobile with 14%.

International Expansion. Although several Colombian companies accepted reinsurance in foreign markets several years ago, this practice has been appreciably reduced because the results have been less than satisfactory. The Colombian Reinsurance Company has maintained important exchanges with good results.

Workmen's Compensation. Three bodies make up the Social Security system: the National Prevention Fund (for government officers), the Colombian Social Insurance Institute (deaths, disease, maternity, workmen's com-

55

pensation, retirement, disability for private workers), and insurance companies which extend their coverage through group policies.

Agents and Brokers. The profession as a whole is regulated and protected through rules on inscription, incompatibilities, restrictions, etc. Recent changes in the Business Code (1972) still leave unsolved differences between agency and broker contracts, which in their commercial and labor aspects are somewhat similar.

Public Insurance. This is conducted through several institutions, including La Previsora, S.A.; El Instituto de Crédito Territorial; the Fondo de Promoción de Exportaciones; the Caja de Crédito Agrario, Industrial y Minero; the Caja Nacional de Previsión; the Instituto Colombiano de Seguros Sociales, etc.

Reinsurance. The Bank Supervisory Office controls reinsurance regarding solvency of reinsurers. No risk may be undertaken which exceeds 20% of the company's capital and reserves. Sixty percent of the total premiums must be retained in the country, which is a requirement of almost all types of insurance.

II. FORM AND OPERATION OF PRIVATE INSURERS

Basic Legal Rules. These rules include the Code of Land Commerce of 1887 (annulled by decree of 27 March 1971, effective 1 January 1972); Stock Companies Law of 23 April 1931; Insurance Company Regulating Law of 15 November 1927; law-decree of 18 August 1940 regarding Insurance Companies; decrees of 17 August 1963 and 25 July 1968 on Insurance Cooperative Societies.

Legal Nature. This exists through corporations or through specialized cooperative societies. The latter, without practical legal status for a long time, are new in the process of acquiring it.

Social Purpose. This is limited exclusively to insurance and reinsurance operations and to the necessary activities for their proper development.

Scope of Operations. A company may deal simultaneously in all forms of insurance whenever requirements of minimum capital and guaranty deposit are met. As a matter of practice the Supervisory Office asks for the formation of separate stock companies for underwriting individual life insurance.

Constitution Requirements. Both national and foreign companies require a minimum capital of 800,000 pesos (about $40,000), totally disbursed. A lesser minimum is considered if companies deal in certain insurance branches, e.g., life—150,000 pesos, transport and fire—200,000 pesos; automobile, airplane, and their damages—100,000 pesos; disease and personal accident— 100,000 pesos. Minimum capital for the remaining branches is 50,000 pesos. Actually, through the use of its discretionary powers, the Supervisory Office demands considerably larger sums as minimums. Such capital is not required of cooperative societies unless they assume the risks of noncooperative groups, in which case the above rules are applied.

Both national and foreign companies are required to disburse a waranty deposit of 300,000 pesos ($15,000) in municipal, department, and government bonds; promisory notes and obligations; as well as securities and shares with mortgage waranty. Companies which do not operate in all risks are granted minor deposits between 25,000 and 100,000 pesos. These deposits will double if the collected net premiums exceed 50,000 pesos in any branch. This capital is not required of cooperatives unless they assume risks of nonmembers, in which case the norms are applied.

Process of Authorization. National companies must present the following documents: a written constitution; social statutes; certificates of possession from the office of directors and managers; technical basis, tariffs and policies and reinsurance contracts that cover risks that may exceed 20% of the social stock.

Foreign companies have the same obligations. In addition they must present a statement of acceptance from the Colombian legislature, a certificate of operation in their native land, nomination of trustees or delegates for Colombia, and any other document that the Supervisory Office requests as proof of solvency and good reputation of the company.

The procedure for both national and foreign companies includes producing the folder processed by the Bank Supervisory Office when dealing with stock companies or by the Cooperative National Supervisory Office when dealing with such companies. The latter also requires Bank Supervisory Office authorization when these companies extend services to persons not affiliated with the Cooperative. Authorization is discretional; denial resolutions may be appealed. Authorization must be recorded in the Public Commerce Register and must be published in the official journal. All certificates of authorization expire annually on 31 December. Application for renewal must be presented before 15 November.

Reporting Obligations. The following documents must be submitted to the Supervisory Office within forty-five days following 30 June and 31 December each year by both national and foreign companies: balance sheets and complementary annex documents, reports on the status of businesses and amount and nature of their risks. The Supervisory Office approves the procedures for reporting.

III. CONTRACTING

Basic Legal Rules. These include the Code of Land Commerce of 1887 modified by decree of 27 March 1970, effective 1 January 1972; Insurance Company Regulating Act of 15 November 1927; and law-decree of 18 August 1940 on Insurance Companies.

Policies. Policies, but not necessarily insurance proposals, require prior approval of the Bank Supervisory Office. Approval is also required to modify general coverage of contracts, which occasionally contain mandatory legal clauses. Sometimes policies contain a predetermined content—e.g., fidelity policy for national employees and policies of fulfillment of contracts subscribed by the nation.

Tariffs. Tariffs must be approved by the Bank Supervisory Office. Applications for tariffs must include technical (actuarial) notes which cannot be modified without authorization of the office. Some tariffs, such as Group Life Insurance, are uniformly fixed by the Supervisory Office.

Compulsory Insurance. By risk category, three types of insurance are required: (1) Fidelity Insurance, established by a law of 10 November 1938 and required for all government employees. It guarantees proper management of monies or other things of value entrusted to or administered by these persons. (2) Civil Transport Liability Insurance of Transporters, established by Decree 1.393 of 1970. It covers all transport vehicles, collective or private, and covers both passengers and loads. (3) Automobile-Civil Liability Insurance, which was created by Decree 1.344 of 1970 but has not been put into effect.

Five types of insurance are required of the companies involved in the insuring: (1) Government Bodies Risks. According to Decree 2.222 of 1962, insurance on national wealth, decentralized public organizations, commissariats, management, etc., must be subscribed with La Previsora S.A., Compañia de Seguros, where the government is a major stock holder through the National Prevention Fund. Profits of this company are reinsured in private companies. (2) Life Group Insurance, handled through the Land Credit Institute, which insures its mortgage debtors to the amount of the debt pending payment. The Institute charges standard premiums for this type of insurance according to the law of 7 December 1945. A mandatory group life insurance for business employees and industrial workers also exists for persons not covered by Social Security. Companies with stock exceeding 100,000 pesos ($5,000) are exempted when they cover this risk directly. (3) Export Credit Insurance. Coverage of political and extraordinary risks is purchased through the Export Promotion Fund which guarantees up to 80% of net loss. Commercial risks are covered through a private company, "Seguros la Union," which deals with this type of guarantee. This company operates under the guidance of the Guaranty Commission which includes representatives of the Export Promotion Fund. (4) Agriculture and Cattle Risks. The Agrarian, Mining, and Industrial Credit Fund handles special insurance cases of this type. Coverage of these risks is actually under study. (5) Social Security. The National Prevention Fund provides social security coverage of public servants. The Colombian Social Insurance covers private employees regarding retirement, incapacity, death, disease, maternity, and social labor insurance. Group insurance is provided by private insurance companies.

Foreign Insurance Restrictions. No risk may be covered in a foreign country unless authorized by the Supervisory Office when no company in Colombia accepts the risk. The penalty for providing coverage without authorization is 50% of the value of the premiums that would have been paid in Colombia.

IV. TECHNICAL RESERVES

Basic Legal Rules. Law of 15 November 1927 regulating insurance companies, decree of 18 July 1960 on investment systems, and decree of 17 August 1963 on cooperative societies.

Classes. Mathematical (life) reserves are called Technical Reserves of Life and Annuity Rent. These are calculated annually by the companies, in concurrence with the Bank Superintendent, and considering the required percentages of the "Colombian Table of Mortality" of 1971. Premium reserves equal 40% of the annual net premiums. Outstanding losses are composed of 100% of pending payments at the end of the fiscal year. Deviations of loss ratio are called "major loss reserves." It accumulates from year to year with its annual increase equal to a percentage of the premiums, normally 5–100% of the reserve of current risks. There also exists an "additional reserve" similar to the previous reserve, also voluntary in nature.

Value Fluctuation is not regulated, although some companies set aside some of their net profits as a reserve for investment protection purposes.

Another type reserve that should be maintained is a legal reserve fund of no less than 20% of the disbursed capital. Ten percent of the profits are allocated to this reserve annually until the required amount has been set aside.

All reserves must be invested in Colombia. Thirty-five percent of the stock and capital reserves and 54% of the technical reserves (25% and 61% respectively in a life insurance company) must be invested in the following manner: (1) 40% in public obligations or securities; (2) 25% in mortgage certificates in mortgage banks; (3) 20% in general guaranty bonds of the Industrial Promotion Institute, financial corporations and other banks, and in bonds of the Agrarian, Industrial and Mining Credit Fund; (4) 15% in mortgage loans for low-income housing and mortgage certificates issued by mortgage banks.

The remainder of the capital and technical reserves is to be invested in (1) organizational expenses of emerging companies (10% limit of disbursed capital), (2) furnishings and equipment for operation (15% limit of disbursed capital and capital reserves), (3) loans guaranteed by insurance policies (up to their redemption value), (4) investments in branches and agencies abroad (25% limit of disbursed capital and capital reserves), (5) securities and public obligations, (6) stock company shares and bonds not associated with insurance and capitalization (10% of capital, capital reserves and technical reserves), (7) shares in insurance and capitalization companies (the minimum legal capital must not be affected), (8) mortgage bank certificates, (9) agrarian and industrial bonds, (10) real estate, (11) mortgage or collateral guarantee loans on real estate, (12) savings and checking accounts in national banks (up to the limit represented by normal quantities for the operation of the company—, (13) other stocks or securities with authorization from the superintendent operation of the company), (13) other stocks or securities with authorization from the superintendent. Regarding investment, cooperative societies are under direct government control.

General Requirements of Goods To Be Used as Reserves Covers. (1) Securities and public obligations, without limitation; (2) General Guaranty Industrial Bonds, issued by financial corporations and banks, must be approved by the Bank Superintendent regarding interests on bonds and loans; (3) mortgage loans for construction of low-income housing can be issued only to persons who have no housing of their own. The quantity of the loan cannot exceed 150,000 pesos ($7,000). Loan interest cannot exceed that established by mortgage banks and the minimum amortization period must be five years.

Investment limits include the following: (1) Investment in securities of one company may not be higher than 10% of the capital and reserves of the investing company and they may not be higher than 25% of the shares issued by one company. (2) Investment in real estate and loans with mortgage guarantee may be no higher than 60% of the capital and reserves of the insuring entity. (3) Investment in real estate may be no higher than 30% of the capital and reserves.

V. REINSURANCE

Basic Legal Rules. These include the law of 15 November 1927 regulating insurance companies, the law-decree of 18 August 1940 on insurance companies, and the Superintendency Resolution of 17 May 1952.

Legal Nature. These must be in the form of stock companies. Cooperatives cannot accept reinsurance.

Authorization Procedures. National or foreign companies authorized to sell insurance are automatically authorized to operate in reinsurance; however, authorization is required to work exclusively in reinsurance. The procedures are the same as those given under "Constitution and Operation of Private Institutions." (Section II). Reinsurance cessions are required for each risk whose value exceeds 20% of the capital stock and reserves of the company.

Reporting requirements are the same as those listed under "Constitution and Operation of Private Institutions" (Section II). No separation between operations of direct insurance and reinsurance is required in the balance sheet. Balances and remittances in foreign currency are controlled by the

Banco de la República. Each company must submit its book of rules to the Superintendency, which grants authorization. Bank checking accounts are authorized in foreign currency for payment and deposit of balances in foreign money.

The Banking Superintendency exercises official control by regulating retentions of individual companies and of the whole national market (60% minimum of premiums issued in each branch except foreign commerce insurance, airplane insurance, insurance for ships and oil pipelines and other goods which, in the judgment of the Superintendency, should be submitted to special treatment).

VI. TAXES

Basic Legal Rules. These include Law 81 of 1960; Decree 437 of 1961 on income tax regulation and complementary; the 1960 Decree 2908 on stamp taxes; the 1963 Law 24 which modifies Decree 2908; the 1971 Decree 435 readjusting stamp and stamped paper taxes; the 1927 Law 105 on control of insurance companies which serves as a foundation for the contribution to expenses of the Banking Superintendency; 1936 Law 63 organizing taxes on inheritance in general, assignations and donations; 1963 Law 21 which modifies Law 63; 1968 Law 33 on industry and commerce taxes.

Taxes and Loadings over Premiums. Stamp taxes are applied on insurance policy premiums, their renewals, supplemental agreements, or appendixes. are 4% for individual life insurance, 3.50% for group life insurance, 5% for general or commercial insurance, 5% for other risks, and 3% on balances of reinsurance accounts abroad. The Banking Superintendency supervision expense contribution is 6.24% of net premiums.

Taxes and Loadings over Profits. Revenue tax is a general type tax on incomes of individuals or corporations. For stock companies, through which insurance companies operate, the tariff is 12% when taxable net profit income does not exceed 100,000 pesos, 24% on the excess above 100,000 but less than 1,000,000, and 36% on excess above 1,000,000. Exempt from taxes are interests on national, departmental or municipal bonds, industrial bonds of the Banco Central Hipotecario, mortgage certificates, stock company dividends, and earnings from selling shares or other securities. Insurance companies also are subject to excess profit taxes but not to property taxes. Individuals receiving dividends are taxed between 0.75 and 52%, depending on the value of the taxed revenue. Certain types of dividends are eligible for exemption.

Other Taxes. Law 33, article 40 of 1968 authorizes municipalities and the Special District of Bogotá to establish industry and commerce taxes on loan and insurance companies with the following maximum tax limits: for towns whose inhabitants do not exceed 50,000, the tax is 3,600 pesos a year;

50,000–150,000, 7,200 pesos a year; 150,000–40,000, 12,000 pesos; more than 40,000, 24,000 pesos; and for the Special District of Bogotá, 36,000 pesos.

Individual or group life insurance, when paid to beneficiaries, are subject to a tax similar to inheritance taxes. The amount of this tax fluctuates between 1 and 26%, depending on the degree of kindred between the beneficiary and the insuree and depending on the amount of insurance. Compulsory group insurance covering social benefits from companies for workers not affiliated with the Colombian Social Security Institute are not taxed.

VII. PRODUCTION (AGENTS)

Basic Legal Rules.   These include the law of 15 November 1927 regulating insurance companies, the law of 15 November 1966 regulating agents' profession, the decree-regulation of 10 May 1967 on agents, the 24 September 1969 resolution on professional training and the new Business Code (articles 1347–1353).

Kinds of Agents.   Agents placing insurance are individuals who, as employees, are representatives of one or more insurance companies, write and alter contracts in a particular territory, either alone or with other agents. General agencies are offices directed by individuals or corporations who through their own organization have exclusive representation in one or more insurance companies in a particular territory. Their duties include collecting premiums, inspecting risks, intervening in salvages, and promoting insurance operations, either directly or through agents representing the companies for which they work.

Previous Requirements.   An agent must be of legal age, a Colombian, or a foreigner with at least a year's residency in Colombia. In addition, an agent must be recorded in the register of the Banking Superintendency, must hold a certificate issued by the Superintendency attesting that he is an agent, and must have received adequate instruction in the branch of operations. Registration with the Banking Superintendency is requested by the insurance company; it expires annually on December 31 and is renewed upon request of the company.

Agencies must be accredited by public deed, and they are required by law to state their minimum assets.

Authorization.   Authorization is granted by the Banking Superintendency, at the advice of the Title Inscription Board. Authorization is discretional and may be denied even though the candidate meets all legal requirements for being an agent.

Surety.   The Superintendency regulates bail since the new Business Code does not specify quantity.

Agency Contract.   This is a work contract regulating the services of a company. It is subject to expiration if the company serviced by the agency does not apply for renewal of authorization from the Superintendency by the end of each year. It cannot reduce the advantages or working conditions of its professional agents. Any discrepancies between the agent and the company are resolved by the Work Courts. The broker's contract has a commercial nature.

Commissions. Commissions are agreed upon by the company and the agent within limits of the work rules. If agents belong to a union, commissions and other contract rules should be agreed upon collectively. Normal commissions are the following: Life, transport, and fire insurance agents receive 20%; general agents and brokers receive 27.50%. Automobile agents receive 10%; general agents and brokers, 15%. Robbery, management and fulfillment (fidelity) agents receive 12.5%; general agents and brokers, 17.50%. The lower percentage for placing agents is compensated for by the fact that they are covered by Social Security benefits through their companies.

Official Protection. A noncompulsory Colombian Insurance Agent Association provides union coverage. The following persons may not be insurance agents: those who have official or semiofficial positions or belong to associated public bodies, except for teachers; directors, managers, administrators, or employees of banking and loan institutions; partners, directors, administrators, or employees of commercial enterprises when insurance premiums of these enterprises or of their clientele exceed 20% of the total premiums obtained annually by the insurance companies they represent.

Insurance companies are forbidden to pay commissions to anyone other than legally authorized agents or agencies. However, commissions can be paid on changes to a policy to a former agent if he was instrumental in issuing the policy and if he is not affected by the incompatibilities cited above.

VIII. INSTITUTIONAL BODIES

There are eleven governmental organizations affecting insurance in Colombia:

1. The Banking Superintendency. This organism is answerable to the president of the republic and controls insurance stock companies in matters concerning their organization, functioning, and decline. It also supervises banks, financial corporations, investment funds, and general deposit warehouses; therefore, it controls the nation's financial system as a whole. The insurance division of the superintendency is manned by a corps of inspectors who visit insurance companies. The Superintendency interprets insurance laws for insurers and insurees, and there is no appeal through governmental routes against its decisions except for a reinstatement recource before the contentious-administrative jurisdiction (the State Council).

2. Consulting Commission of Insurance is a body associated with the

Banking Superintendency to advise the superintendent in all insurance matters. This body also analyzes and proposes changes on existing legislation and on the issuing of reports on policies, tariffs, and commissions of agents submitted to its consideration by the Superintendency.

3. Consulting Council of Actuaries integrates its activities with the Superintendency in problems related to life insurance.

4. The National Superintendency of Cooperatives is a parallel body to the Banking Superintendency regarding insurance cooperatives. The National Superintendency controls actuation.

5. The Title Inscription Board is an auxiliary organ of the Banking Superintendency regarding the study of applications for the recording of agents in the register. The Superintendent heads the body which is comprised of the insurance company and the authorized agents' representatives. This body also maintains a credentials register for agents and instructions for cancellation proceedings.

6. The Territorial Credit Institute is the official body responsible for the coverage of group life insurance for its debtors.

7. Mining, Industrial and Agrarian Loan Bank is the official and exclusive body responsible for risk coverage of agricultural products and livestock, particularly nonpayment risks in the amortization of credits issued by the Loan Bank itself. Insurance operations undertaken by this body are exempt from taxes and contributions.

8. La Previsora, S.A., Insurance Company is a private rights body owned by the state which is exclusively responsible for diverse type risks affecting the interests of the nation and of official organizations.

9. National Prevention Fund is a public rights body responsible for the coverage of occupational accidents insurance and for the social benefits of the state administration functionaries.

10. Colombian Social Insurance Institute is a public rights body responsible for the coverage of illness, maternity, work accidents, disability, age, and death of private employees.

11. Exports Promotion Fund is administered by the Banco de la República under supervision of the Superintendency. It is responsible for coverage of political and unusual risks in foreign trade.

Six associations affect insurance in Colombia:

1. Colombian Association of Insurance Companies (ASECOLDA) is a private rights body whose main purpose is the coordination and defense of interests of affiliated bodies (practically the entire market). It studies and proposes to the Banking Superintendency tariffs and policy terms for most branches. It is represented in the Consulting Commission of Insurance. See paragraph (2) of the preceding section. ASECOLDA undertakes important studies on technical aspects of insurance activities and carries out functions related to the legal professional qualifications of insurance companies. It also promotes publicity campaigns of an institutional nature.

2. Colombian Association of Insurance Agents (ACODASE) is a trade union body which defends the interests of insurance agents. It intervenes in contract agreements with insurers. Membership is not compulsory.

3. The Insurance Studies Center provides courses for insurance company employees and agents in Bogotá and other Colombian cities.

4. Colombian Association of Actuaries is a private association. It studies insurance activities and defends the interests of its associates. It acts as an adviser to the Superintendency and to ASECOLDA.

5. The Colombian Association of Insurance Brokers is a private guild association of insurance brokers which serves the needs of its members.

6. The Colombian Association of Insurance Law is a private body, a member of the International Association of Insurance Law (AIDA). Its members are lawyers connected with insurance activities. It conducts studies related to rights and insurance contracts.

IX. CHARACTERISTICS OF THE SIXTIES

1. Liberalization of Reserve Investments. Decree 1.691 of 1960 established high-level obligatory investments, limiting the financial activities of insurance companies which have continued requesting its modification, especially regarding capital reserves.

2. Suspension of authorization of New Companies. The Banking Superintendency has limited the establishment of both new national companies and foreign agencies or company branches.

3. Creation of La Previsora, S.A. By a decree of 4 August 1962 (regulated by resolutions of February and March, 1963) La Previsora, S.A. Insurance Company was organized with the state as major stockholder. It is responsible for coverage of risks related to the interests of national and official organizations and in this respect, it is a monopoly.

4. Regulation of Insurance Production. In 1966 the law regulating the profession of insurance agents was published, regulated by the 10 May 1967 decree and complemented by the 24 September 1969 resolution on professional qualifications. These dispositions, embellished by the 27 March 1971 decree which modified important aspects of the Commerce Code of 1969, assumes ample regulation of the activities of placing agents and insurance brokers.

5. Development of Group Life Insurance. The development of this kind of coverage, whose promotion originated from the official tariffs created in 1958 (March 17 resolution), was initiated at the beginning of the decade. In 1967 the Colombian Mortality Tables were published, updating the 1957 tables.

6. Introduction of Compulsory Traffic Risk Insurance. Although its establishment did not occur in the sixties, its importance makes it worthwhile to cite here. The Compulsory Civil Responsibility Transporters Insurance (De-

cree 1.393 of 1970) although still unenforced, covers civil responsibility risks from traffic activities.

7. Creation of Consulting Organisms. By resolutions of 3 March 1967 and 18 June 1969, the Advisory Commission on Insurance and the Advisory Council of Actuaries were created to aid the Superintendency with technical research and advice.

8. Professional Qualification. Important work in the area of training professionals for a career in insurance is undertaken through the Professional Insurance and Reinsurance College, through the recent creation of postgraduate courses by the Insurance Department of the University of Bogotá, through encouragement by the Colombian Association of Insurance Companies (ASECOLDA), and the establishment of insurance courses in various institutions.

9. State-owned Social Security Insurance. The creation of the Colombian Social Security Institute provided coverage for old age, disability, death, and work accidents formerly provided by private insurance companies.

X. FUNDAMENTAL LEGISLATION

Chronological Order

12 October 1869—Land Commerce Code (Law 57, 1.887).

15 November 1927—Regulating law on Insurance Companies (No. 105).
23 April 1931—Stock Company law.

10 November 1938—Regulating law on Management and Fidelity Insurance (No. 225).

27 June 1939—Decree-regulation of the Management and Fidelity Insurance (No. 1.348).

18 July 1940—Decree-law on Insurance Companies (No. 1.403).

18 July 1940—Regulating decree on Mining Credit Insurance (No. 1.403).

24 March 1941—Regulating decree on Mining Credit Insurance (No. 576).

7 December 1945—Regulating law on Mortgagors' Group Insurance (No. 29).

23 January 1946—Resolution-regulation of the Mortgagors' Group Insurance (No. 718b).

27 July 1950—Regulating Decree of Stock Companies.

17 May 1952—Resolution regulating reinsurance (No. 151).

24 April 1953—Resolution with new regulations on Mortgagors Group Insurance (No. 279).

12 July 1954—Decree regulating the Mining Loan Bank (No. 2.102).

30 November 1954—Resolution regulating the management and fulfillment insurance policy (No. 1.323).

22 June 1955—Decree on Insurance Statutes Section of the Agrarian, Industrial, and Mining Loan Bank (No. 1.697).

14 May 1956—Resolution with additions to the Management and Fidelity Insurance Policy (No. 1.573).

17 March 1958–Resolution on group life insurance tariffs (No. 44).

7 August 1959–Resolution on Colombian Mortality Tables (No. 729).

18 July 1960–Decree on Investment Procedures (No. 1.691).

4 August 1962–Decree regulating La Previsora S.A., Insurance Company (No. 2.222).

14 February 1963–Resolution-regulation on La Previsora S.A., Insurance Company (No. 2.212).

14 March 1963–Resolution regulation on La Previsora S.A., Insurance Company (No. 2.217).

17 July 1963–Decree on Insurance Cooperatives (No. 1.598).

15 November 1966–Law regulating agents (No. 65).

3 May 1967–Resolution creating the Insurance Advisory Commission (No. 88).

10 May 1967–Decree-regulation on agents (No. 837).

4 November 1967–Resolution on the 1962 Colombian Mortality Table (No. 512).

25 July 1968–Decree-regulation on insurance cooperatives (No. 2.059).

18 June 1969–Resolution creating the Actuaty Advisory Council (No. 856).

24 September 1969–Resolution on professional qualifications (agents) (No. 1.597).

27 March 1971–Decree modifying the Commerce Code (forseeable effective date, 1 January 1972).

By Subject

General Dispositions–Land Commerce Code, 12 October 1869; Law regulating insurance companies, 15 November 1927; Stock Company Law, 23 April 1931; Decree-law on insurance companies, 18 July 1940; Decree regulating stock companies, 27 July 1950; Decree on investment procedures, 18 July 1960; decree on insurance cooperatives, 17 July 1963; decree-regulation on insurance cooperatives, 25 July 1968; decree modifying the Commerce Code, 27 May 1971.

Management and Fidelity Insurance–regulating law, 10 November 1938; decree-regulation, 27 June 1939; resolution regulating the policy, 30 November 1954; resolution with additions to the policy, 14 May 1956.

Mining Credit Insurance–regulating decree, 18 July 1940; regulating decree, 24 March 1941; regulating decree of the Loan Bank, 12 July 1954; decree on statutes of the Insurance Section of the Mining, Industrial, and Agrarian Loan Bank, 22 June 1955.

Mortgagors' Group Insurance–Regulating law 7 December 1945; resolution-regulation, 23 January 1946; resolution with new regulation 23 April 1953.

Life Insurance–Resolution on group insurance tariffs, 17 March 1958; resolution on 1957 Colombian Mortality Tables, 1 July 1959; resolution on 1962 Colombian Mortality Tables, 4 November 1967.

Reinsurance—Regulating resolution, 17 May 1952.

Agents—Regulating law, 14 November 1966; decree-regulation, 10 May 1967; resolution on professional qualifications, 24 September 1969.

Insurance Advisory Commission—Resolution creating commission, 3 March 1967.

Actuary Advisory Council—Resolution creating council, 18 June 1967.

La Previsora, Insurance Company—Regulating decree, 4 August 1962; resolution-regulation, 14 February 1963; resolution-regulation, 14 March 1963.

Ecuador

I. GENERAL INFORMATION

Historical Note. The first national insurance company, Ecuadorian Fire Insurance Company, was organized in 1886. The Guayaquil National Insurance Company was founded the following year. Foreign companies, the North British and Mercantile Insurance Co. and the London Union Assurance Society, etc., were in operation prior to this time. A major fire in Guayaquil in October 1896 caused the bankruptcy of both national companies and a large economic loss for the foreign ones.

Official Control. The first law on insurance control was enacted in 1936; it was later incorporated into the Code of Commerce. Insurance is regulated through the Bank Supervisory Office, an autonomous and independent entity which also controls finance companies, stock companies, and mutual societies.

Professional Statute. The major representative bodies include the Insurance Companies Chamber, where affiliation is voluntary, and the Brokers Agents Unions. There are also insurance pools in the fire insurance branch.

Market Structure. The market is composed of twenty-one companies, eleven of them national companies and the remainder foreign companies. These companies represent 37% of the total volume of the market. Important branches include life, fire, and automobile, which represent 59% of the collections of the country.

International Expansion. No national company operates in a foreign country.

Workmen's Compensation. Insurance companies operate in a free market on a competitive basis. The Ecuadorian Social Security covers these risks for all its affiliates.

Agents and Brokers. Broker agents serve as intermediaries in insurance production through a labor contract with one or more insurance companies. Employment agencies operate in a free way through their own organization and may insure with any company.

Public Insurance. No public insurancy exists on the Ecuadorian market.

Reinsurance. No national reinsurance companies exist. All direct transactions are reinsured abroad.

II. FORM AND OPERATION OF PRIVATE INSURERS

Basic Legal Rules. These include: Law on Companies, codification of 15 November 1971; Insurance Companies General Law of 17 July 1865, codification of 13 March 1967; Code of Commerce in reference to maritime insurance, and Cooperative Societies Law of 7 September 1966.

Legal Nature. This includes stock companies and cooperative societies.

Social Purpose. This is limited exclusively to insurance and reinsurance operations.

Operations Area. A company may operate in all lines of insurance simultaneously provided minimum stock requirements have been met.

Constitution Requirements. National and foreign companies must make a deposit of 1,500,000 sucres ($60.000) to deal in life insurance and the same amount to deal in diverse branches of insurance excluding life. The stock must be 3,000,000 sucres for a company dealing in life and other kinds of insurance.

A "reserve fund" is required for both national and foreign companies. Although a warranty deposit in the strictest sense does not exist, the "reserve fund" must be comprised of no less than 50% of the disbursed capital. Ten percent of the net profits from each fiscal year must be assigned to this fund.

Process of Authorization. National companies must introduce statutes known as "social contract minutes" before the Bank Supervisory Office when applying for authorization. Once authorization is granted, these companies must present a written constitution plus policy rules, certificates, premium invoices, and tariffs to the Office. When the company deals in life insurance, it must also present technical notes.

Foreign companies must state which insurance lines they are planning to sell; site of the principal office, agencies, and branches; the name of the general trustee for Ecuador; a certificate proving they have operated for at least five years in their homeland and that they are authorized by their country's authorities to operate in foreign countries. Once authorized, besides the documents that are required from national companies, foreign companies must present legal powers conferred on their representative, a copy of their by-laws and of their written constitution, and a copy of the insurance act under which they operate in their own country.

To gain authorization both national and foreign companies must present their portfolios to the Bank Supervisory Office. When legal requirements are met, authorization is mandatory. Authorization must be recorded in the Commerce Register and in the Mercantile Register. It must be published in a newspaper of wide circulation and in the Official Register.

A resolution denying authorization must show cause, and it may be appealed before the Supreme Court of Justice. A certificate of authorization from the Supervisory Office is required before a company may begin operations in each type of insurance. If no business is executed within six months, authorizations to establish or operate are revoked.

Reporting Requirements. Both national and foreign companies must present monthly reports to the superintendent on the development of their businesses. The Supervisory Office establishes the rules for bookkeeping.

III. CONTRACTING

Basic Legal Rules. These include General Law of Insurance Companies of 15 July 1965 and the codification of 13 March 1967; Decree on Insurance Companies of 29 November 1963; Code of Commerce regarding Marine Insurance, and Law of Cooperatives societies, 7 September 1966.

Policies. Policies for life insurance and most other risks are submitted individually by each company for approval; however, fire and transport policies established by the Supervisory Office are common to the total market.

Tariffs. There are no exclusive or compulsory tariffs. However, the Bank Supervisory Office approves tariffs and their modifications.

Compulsory Insurances. The only compulsory insurance covers civil responsibility in the event of automobile accidents.

Foreign Insurance Restrictions. The following types of insurance may not be subscribed in foreign countries: (1) personal insurance when the insured individual is in Ecuador at the time of the signing of the contract, (2) insurance covering fire and other risks on property located in Ecuador, (3) insurance covering air or ships' hulls when ships are registered in Ecuador, (4) Other types of insurance against risks that may occur in Ecuador. The above-mentioned types of insurance may be purchased abroad if no authorized Ecuadorian company will provide for it and if the Supervisory Office gives approval.

IV. TECHNICAL RESERVES

Basic Legal Rules. These include the General Insurance Company Law of 15 July 1965 and diverse resolutions on mathematical reserves and current risks established by the Bank Superintendency.

Classes. The mathematical constitution will be calculated in accordance with the mortality rate and with the technical interest rate established by the Superintendency. Other rates which provide similar or better results may be used providing the technical interest rate does not exceed 4% annually.

Companies providing general insurance and all companies whose responsibility expires annually must maintain a premium reserve of at least 40% of the net premiums received during the year. Deducted from this reserve is the value of the ceded reinsurance premiums if they are no more than the sums resulting from applying the so-called "twenty-fourths" method. For companies whose accepted reinsurance movement is greater than that of ceded reinsurance, the reserve held by ceders is deducted from the value of the first. For insurances covering transport and other risks (except individual life and life pension income where premiums are paid monthly), the reserve may be reduced to a third of the net premiums received in the last quarter of the fiscal year; however, if during the last quarter premiums come in in December only, the reserve shall be comprised of the total net premiums received in that month.

Outstanding losses are called "reserves for pending obligations." They are calculated as follows: (1) for disasters to be covered—the probable value of their amount, (2) for liquidated disasters to be paid—the value of liquidation, (3) for expiration of dowery policies and dividends of insurees—their nominal value.

Deviations of loss ratio and value fluctuations are not expressly regulated.

Investment is common to all types of technical reserves and must be made in the following areas: (1) Securities of the Values Commission, National Financial Corporation, (2) mortgage certificates of development system credit banks, mortgage banks, or mortgage sections of commercial banks, (3) state bonds, municipal bonds, or Ecuadorian Housing Bank bonds, (4) banking or insurance company stock shares, (5) fiduciary securities and shares of finance companies, (6) first mortgage loans on urban real estate, (7) loans to life insurees, (8) income from urban buildings or urban sites for building, and (9) savings banks or deposits in banks of the country.

General Requirements of Goods To Be Used as Reserve Covers. The investment in mortgage certificates issued by banks or in shares of stock of bank companies or insurance is possible only when these companies have paid dividends within the past three years. Investments in securities of other types of stock companies or in real estate must have prior approval of the Bank Superintendency.

Limits of Investment. Investment in securities of the Values Commission must represent a minimum of total capital, reserves fund, and technical reserves. Investment in the Ecuadorian Housing Bank bonds may not exceed 10%. Loans to insurees with life policies may not exceed the respective redemption values. Investments in first mortgage loans on urban real estate and urban income property (buildings), or urban building sites may not exceed 50%. Investment in savings banks and bank deposits may not exceed 10%. The Bank Superintendency may authorize investment in foreign life policy reserves issued in foreign currency, with a 15% limit of total mathematical reserves.

V. REINSURANCE

Basic Legal Rules. The General Insurance Company Law of 15 July 1965 governs reinsurance.

Legal Nature. Stock companies and cooperative companies are the only forms authorized to conduct reinsurance transactions.

Process of Authorization. This is similar to that set forth in section II under "Constitution and Operation of Private Institutions." Companies operating in reinsurance only also are subject to capital and guarantee deposits established for direct insurers.

Reporting Obligations. Insurance companies must submit ceded and accepted reinsurance contracts plus all their changes for the approval of the Superintendent.

Balances and Remittances in Foreign Currency. These must submit to Monetary Board Regulations since exchange control has been in existence since June 1970.

Official Control. This control is exercised by the Superintendency in the same manner as for direct insurance companies. Foreign companies may not contract reinsurance in their home offices.

VI. TAXES

Basic Legal Rules. These include the General Insurance Company Law of 15 July 1965, the Cooperative Law of 7 September 1966, and the Stamp Law of 17 January 1966.

Taxes and Loadings Over Premiums. The Stamp Tax sets up the following encumberances: general insurance, 5%; life, 7% in the first year and 2% in following years. A contribution of 2.50% of all premiums finances Bank Superintendency costs.

Taxes and Loadings over Profits. This includes a 1% contribution for foundling homes.

VII. PRODUCTION (AGENTS)

Basic Legal Rules. These include the General Insurance Company Law of 15 July 1965 and the Regulation on the Bank Superintendency of 15 August 1969.

Kinds of Agents. An insurance broker agent is a person who has a contract with one or more insurance companies and is dedicated to the insurance profession. A policy-writing agency is dedicated to the furthering of insurance activities in one sector or in the whole country but has no affiliation with a particular company.

Previous Requirements. Agents and agencies must be Ecuadorian citizens who are fit to conduct business. The same holds true for persons of foreign nationality, who must live in Ecuador. Broker agents must complete a six-month trial period and must have sold a maximum of five life policies (for a total insured capital of at least 200,000 sucres) and another five policies in general risks (with a minimum total premiums of 10,000 sucres).

Authorization. The Superintendency, at the request of insurance companies, grants authorization once the stated prerequisites have been met.

Surety. No regulation concerns bail.

Agency Contracts. Broker agents have labor-type contracts and agencies have commercial contracts. Both must be in writing and must be approved by the Superintendency.

Retribution Commissions.   No regulation covers this area.

Official Protection.   No regulations cover associations or portfolio rights. Persons employed by or associated with the Superintendency and former employees of insurance companies may not be agents or agencies. Insurance agent brokers are considered private employees of the companies and, as such, are subject to Social Security benefits and are protected by the Work Code.

VIII. INSTITUTIONAL BODIES

Government Agencies.   The Bank Superintendency is an autonomous and independent entity responsible for supervising the fulfillment of legislation on private insurance through the Insurance Administration.

Associations.   Four types of associations are recognized in Ecuador: (1) Association of Insurance Companies in Ecuador, which existed until the Chamber of Insurance Companies was created under the General Law of Insurance Companies. (2) Chamber of Insurance Companies in Ecuador supplants the former Association of Insurance Companies in Ecuador but maintains the same functions. It is a voluntary organization of insurance companies and has its own laws and regulations. (3) Agents' unions are labor-type associations made up of insurance agents. They function in accordance with the Work Code. (4) Chamber of Insurers is a cooperative association whose statutes were approved by agreements of 28 October and 19 December 1966.

IX. CHARACTERISTICS OF THE SIXTIES

Outstanding features in the field of insurance in Ecuador in the sixties include the publication of the decree regulating insurance contracts in 1963, the enforcement of the General Law of Insurance Companies in 1965, the promulgation of the Cooperatives Law of 1966, and the regulation on the Bank Superintendency in 1969.

X. FUNDAMENTAL LEGISLATION

Chronological Order

29 November 1963—Decree on Insurance Contracts

15 July 1965—General Law on Insurance Companies

17 January 1966—Law on Stamps

7 September 1966—Law on Cooperatives

13 March 1967—General Law on Insurance Companies (codification)

15 August 1969—Regulation on Banks Supervisory Office

By Subject

General Dispositions include (1) General Law on Insurance Companies, 15 July 1965; (2) Law on Cooperatives, 7 September 1966; (3) General Law on Insurance Companies, 13 March 1967; (4) Law on Companies (codification), 15 February 1971.

Contracting—Decree on Insurance Contracting, 29 November 1963.

Taxes—Law on Stamps, 17 January 1966.

Production (Agents)—Resolution on Banks Supervisory Office, 15 August 1969.

Mexico

I. GENERAL INFORMATION

Historical Note. The eighteenth and nineteenth centuries saw the rise of insurance companies in Mexico, primarily to cover marine risks. The first acts governing insurance are in the Code of Commerce of 1854, with later codes containing regulations controlling various branches of insurance. Near the end of the nineteenth century only foreign companies, mostly English and North American ones, provided insurance.

The first law affecting insurance companies was published in 1892 and took effect on 1 January 1893. This law requires a company to obtain immovable property in Mexico or depositing cash or bonds in the National Treasury or the Bank of Mexico. By 1897 the companies providing fire insurance formed the Mexican Association of Fire Insurance Agents, a compulsory tariff, and maximum commission for agents.

The Insurance Department of the Secretary of the Treasury was created in 1910 to govern insurance activities. Some of its inspection duties, however, were carried out by the National Insurance Commission, also under the Secretary of the Treasury. Also by this time a law governing the organization of insurance companies was in effect.

By 1937 the primary insurance laws in force today, such as the General Law of Insurance Institutions and the Law of the Insurance Contract, were in effect. In 1942 the state created the company, Aseguradora Mexicana, S.A., to provide insurance against loss or damage. In 1946 the Mexican Association of Insurance Companies and a new branch of life insurance merged to create the Mexican Association of Insurance Institutions.

Official Control. The Secretary of the Treasury and Public Credit is the controlling organ for insurance operations; however, the functions of control and inspection of insurance companies are delegated to the National Banking and Insurance Commission.

Professional Statute. Professionalism is provided through two organizations: the Mexican Association of Insurance Institutions which is composed of insurance companies operating in the country, and the Mexican Association of Technical Insurance and Surety Agents, a private group which does not have compulsory membership.

Market Structure. The Mexican market is composed of fifty-eight national companies; fifty of these operate in various branches; six are mutual societies operating in life, life and fire, or fire and agricultural; and two are reinsurance companies. Life insurance is the most important branch, representing approximately a third of the total market. Fire insurance represents 24% of the market, motor vehicle 21%, and the remaining 22% is distributed among the other branches of private insurance.

International Expansion. Little international expansion has occurred except for operations of some companies in the United States relating to motor vehicle and motor third party insurance for tourists traveling in Mexico and for small-scale operations in some Central American countries. Foreign trade in general has increased during the past decade and may have an influence on insurance expansion.

Workmen's Compensation. The compulsory workmen's compensation is included in the Social Security law; however, if collective contracts establish payments greater than the benefits of Social Security, the surplus can be covered by private companies.

Agents and Brokers. A bylaw for agents enacted in 1955 established two classes of agents: general trustees who have extensive powers, and trustees who have restricted powers.

Public Insurance. Social Security, covered by the Mexican Institute of Social Security, provides coverage for workmen's compensation, occupational illnesses, other illnesses and maternity, disability, old age, death, and retirement. Other risks covered by the state include complete agricultural and livestock insurance through the Aseguradora Nacional Agrícola y Ganadera, S.A. and life insurance for state employees through Aseguradora Mexicana S.A. and the Aseguradora Hidalgo S.A.

Reinsurance. Although two professional reinsurance companies (Sociedad Anónima de Reaseguros Alianza and Reaseguradora Patria S.A.) exist, the market is limited since direct insurance companies deal with very little foreign business.

II. FORM AND OPERATION OF PRIVATE INSURERS

Basic Legal Rules. These include the Code of Commerce of 15 September 1889, the Mercantile Societies Law of 4 August 1934; the General Law of Insurance Institutions of 21 August 1935.

Legal Nature. This is provided through joint stock companies or mutual societies.

Social Purpose. A company must be limited to operations of insurance or reinsurance.

Operations Area. Every type of insurance or reinsurance operation is authorized if the company complies with the minimum capital requirements.

Constitution Requirements. Minimum stock for both national and foreign companies is fixed by the Secretary of the Treasury and Public Credit and includes the following limits: Life—2–6 million pesos ($160,000–$480,000), accidents and illness—500,000–1,500,000 pesos, damages—1–2 million pesos if operating in one branch, 2–4 million if operating in two branches, and 3–6 million if operating in three or more branches.

The warrant deposit for national and foreign companies is 10% of the minimum capital in cash or securities suitable for charging against reserves. (See section IV). This deposit is returned if the required authorization is refused or when the registration is confirmed and operations are begun.

In addition, foreign companies are answerable with all their goods and properties including those outside of Mexico. Foreign branch offices or delegations may not be formed.

Process of Authorization. The documentation procedure requires that national companies present constitutional documents, statutes and regulations, technical bases, rates and policies, accounting documents, and the system for distributing dividends to the insured. In addition to the above, foreign companies must declare that they are subject to Mexican laws and jurisdiction, show certification for operation in the home country during the past five years, and designate a representative with power of attorney in Mexico.

The procedure for both national and foreign companies includes obtaining discretional authorization by the federal government through the Secretary of the Treasury and Public Credit following a hearing before the National Banking Commission on Insurance and Sureties. No appeal exists for rejection.

Both national and foreign companies must use the following procedure to become authorized to operate: The Secretary of the Treasury and Public Credit determines the proceedings; discretional authorization is granted by the Secretary following a hearing of the National Banking Commission on Insurance and Sureties. If authorization is denied, there is no appeal. Next, the authorization is recorded in the Public Register of Commerce, and complementary permission is granted by the Secretary of the Treasury and Public Credit. Authorization is granted for operations in life, accident and illness, and damages; in addition, authorization may be granted for reinsurance exclusively. This authorization is published in the official bulletin of the nation.

Reporting Obligation. National companies must submit to the Secretary of the Treasury and Public Credit the following forms: (1) each January the balance sheet, profit and loss account, the valuation book (for life insurance companies), and a statement of settled and pending losses; (2) during the first quarter a general report on each branch of insurance; (3) during the first ten days each month a report on movement of investments. Each year the company must publish within the first four months the general balance sheet of the previous fiscal year in the official bulletin of the nation and in a daily newspaper of leading circulation. The same holds true for foreign companies except that they may publish accounting details for the Mexican branch office only.

III. CONTRACTING

Basic Legal Rules. These include the general law of insurance institutions of 31 August 1935, the Insurance Contract Law of 31 August 1935, and the Code of Commerce of 15 September 1889.

Policies. The office of the Secretary of the Treasury must approve all policies, particularly general conditions, special and additional clauses, individual certificates of group insurance, certificates of policies covered, propositions and applications for insurance, and models of medical examination forms and questionnaires. In reality, these forms are the same for all companies.

Tariffs. The Secretary of the Treasury must approve all rates, including premiums of each branch and the methods used for their calculation. The Secretary may change the rate when he deems it necessary. Except in life and personal injury, rates of premiums are the same for all companies; they are uniform in group life policies.

Compulsory Insurances. Because of the risk involved, travel insurance was established in 1933 to provide compensation up to 50,000 pesos ($4,000) in accidents causing death, permanent or temporary disability, or surgery for persons traveling in public transport. The premium is included in the price of the ticket. Payment depends on the carrier; some carriers have self-insurance funds and others arrange coverage through an insurance company.

Two types of insurance must be obtained through national companies. (1) The complete agricultural and live stock insurance was established in 1961 to provide compensation for agricultural risks (drought, frost, hailstorm, hurricane, fire, plague, dampness, and flooding) and live stock (death by accident or illness, loss of functional capacity, or sickness of animals). The Aseguradora Nacional Agrícola y Ganadera, S.A., backed by the federal government to the extent of 50%, provides this insurance. The maximum insurable capital is 70% of the expected harvest and 90% of the commercial value of the live stock. This insurance can be covered by private mutual societies if they have the permission of the Secretary of the Treasury, participate in the guarantee capital of the Aseguradora Nacional Agrícola y Ganadera, S.A., and reinsure in this company all directly covered risks. (2) Risks of all official organizations, including federal, state, district, municipal governments, federal territories governments, local establishments, societies of mixed state and private ownership, and autonomous commissions must contract their insurance with Aseguradora Mexicana, S.A.

Foreign Insurance Restrictions. It is prohibited to sign contracts with foreign companies for the following: (1) personal insurance when the insured is in Mexico at the time of signing the contract; (2) insurance of goods that are transported from Mexico to other countries or vice versa, when risks are left with persons living in Mexico; (3) insurance of hulls of marine vessels or aircraft or any type of vehicle against risks typical of wet marine insurance or transport insurance when these vessels are of Mexican ownership or are licensed in Mexico; (4) credit insurance when the insured is subject to Mexican legislation; (5) third-party risks insurance from events which could occur in Mexico; (6) insurance of other branches of damages (except life, accident, illness) against risks that could occur in Mexican territory. However, if no insurance company authorized to operate in Mexico can or chooses to deal in the proposed insurance operation, the Secretary of the Treasury may discretionally grant specific authorization for a foreign company to sell insurance through a Mexican insurer. If insurance is contracted in foreign currency, there are limitations on the investment of the technical reserves.

IV. TECHNICAL RESERVES

Basic Legal Rules.   These are the general law of insurance companies of 31 August 1935 and the Investment of Reserves Decree of 31 December 1947.

Classes.   In Mexico these are included under the general title of current risks. In life insurances with a constant premium and increasing risk, the mathematical class will be determined by the average premium reserve (average of the net level premium, but not below the level determined by preliminary term) of policies in force at the time of valuation, subtracted from the deferred net premiums. For renewable short-term insurances, the mathematical class will be determined by the unearned premiums existing at the time of valuation. In both cases, use will be made of the "American experience" tables or any other of equal or greater value. The Rutherfords Annuity Tables or another of greater value must be used for policies of income insurance. For industrial life insurance policies, the Standard Industrial Mortality Tables or others of greater value, or any table proposed by a company based on experience and approved by the Secretary of the Treasury, may be used.

In accidents, illnesses, and damages insurance, premium reserve will be constituted by 45% of the premiums issued during the year after cancellations and devolutions and after deducting 45% of premiums pending collection.

All reserves must be invested in Mexico, with few exceptions. Investments may be made in the following ways: (1) self-retained premiums for operational reserves for reinsurance, for the part retained by the assigner; (2) a minimum of 25% in bonds and securities issued by the federal government, federal district and national institutions of credit, or shares issued by local federal public organizations; (3) up to 30% in mortgage certificates and guaranteed bonds or bonds issued by credit institutions; (4) up to 20% in shares and obligations of Mexican companies; (5) loans with pledged guarantee based on items in numbers 2, 3, and 4 above (with number 2, the limit of investment is 20% and with number 3 it is 30%); (6) loans guaranteed with average premium reserves; (7) up to 30% in mortgage loans on urban properties; (8) up to 30% in urban properties in national territories; (9) property shareholdings in urban property trust in Mexico, (10) up to 10% in cash or bank deposits open to inspection by credit institutions; (11) renewal premiums pending collection; (12) up to 20% in credits, discounts and rediscounts of credit institutions and of permanent development funds for national credit institutions; (13) a minimum of 5% in savings and loan housing programs or mortgage loans on such properties, or in bonds of the same type.

Outstanding losses are known as "Reserves for obligations pending collection" and are classified in two ways: (1) by expired policies and losses which are constituted by an amount equal to the total of pending obligations, and (2) by dividends in deposit constituted by the amount of accumulated interests to the date of valuation.

These monies must be invested in values which, in the opinion of the Secretary of the Treasury, are easy to convert. In cases of pending fixed term obligations, they can be invested in various properties which must also be determined by the Secretary.

Fluctuation of values is included in the general section of "provident fund for value fluctuations and statistical discrepancies." For life insurance, this is constituted in 1% of premiums paid during the year after deducting those invested in reinsurance. If 10% of the net profits is greater than the cited sum, this 10% must be designated as reserve, which must increase annually until it reaches 10% of the average premium reserve plus 25% of the renewable short-term insurance premiums.

In other branches of insurance, fluctuation of values is constituted with 3% of premiums of policies issued during the year minus those ceded in reinsurance, the devolutions and cancellations. If 20% of net profits is greater than the cited amount, this 20% must be constituted as reserve. The reserve must increase annually till it reaches an amount equal to that of the minimum capital or 30% of the self-retained net premiums if the amount of this percentage is greater than the minimum capita.

All monies shall be invested in properties, titles, or values stated in numbers 2, 10, and 12 above.

There are also other reserves, whose constitution and calculation will be determined in each case by the Secretary of the Treasury to guarantee payment of benefits to the insured when these persons have dangerous occupations or are suffering from some illness at the time the contract is made or the contract establishes additional benefits.

General Requirements of Goods To Be Used as Reserve Covers. Shares and obligations of Mexican companies may not be those of mining, petroleum or other insurance companies and must be authorized by the National Commissions of Values which approves titles issued by local federation authorities. Mortgage loans on urban properties must be authorized by the Secretary of the Treasury and must not have a deferment greater than ten years (or fifteen years in the case of urban properties used as housing). Certificates of participation in trust properties must be issued in accordance with the General Law of Titles and Credit Operations. Premiums pending collection must not have been due for more than thirty days and are only to be used for reserves for life insurance companies.

General Limits of Investment. Loans with pledged guarantee mentioned in notes 2, 3, and 4 under investment above must not exceed 80% of the value of the security. Loans guaranteed by the average premium reserve must not exceed the total of the corresponding reserve. Mortgage loans on urban properties must not exceed 50% of the value of the properties (or 65% in the case of properties destined for dwellings). Investments in only one property shall not exceed the limit placed by the National Banking Commission on Insurance and Surety. Investments referred to in notes 3, 7, and 9 above may not exceed 50% of the reserves. The Secretary of the Treasury may authorize investment in foreign securities of reserves equalling obligations in foreign currency, to a maximum of 25% of the total reserves.

V. REINSURANCE

Basic Legal Rule. This is the general law of insurance institutions of 31 August 1935.

Legal Nature. Joint stock companies and mutual societies or a consortium deal in reinsurance.

Process of Authorization. It is the same as that established for companies operating in direct insurance (See section II). Reinsurance operations may not be practiced by subsidiaries or branches of companies which have contracted the direct insurance, just as a company that has contracted the direct insurance may not reinsure with companies of which it is a subsidiary or branch. Surpluses above the limits of net retention for each risk may be ceded to authorized companies. A company may cede in quotas or in second surplus to unauthorized companies, but in the second surplus cannot be of a value above that of the first surplus except when limits of net retention have been exhausted. Then the noncovered surplus may be placed freely, including in foreign countries. In life, accident, illness, third party, professional risks, marine, agricultural transport, and credit risks, there are no reinsurance limits in Mexico or abroad.

Reporting Obligations. These are the same as those set for companies operating in direct insurance (see section II).

Balances and Remittances in Foreign Currency. Because of free currency conversion and the lack of official control in this respect, any excess of a reinsurance account due to cessions or retrocessions abroad can be paid by Mexican companies.

Official Control. This is provided by the Secretary of the Treasury and Public Credit similarly to the manner for direct insurance (see section II).

VI. TAXES

Basic Legal Rules. These are the general law of insurance institutions of 31 August 1935 and the federal law of the tax on premiums received as of 31 December 1947.

Taxes and Loadings over Premiums. The federal tax on premiums affects the total of the premiums, additional premiums, and loadings received by insurance companies in direct insurance operations, according to the following tariffs: 1.5% for insurance covering life or agricultural risks or guaranty life annuity or pension certificates; 5.5% for maritime, transport, or fire branches; 2.8% for personal accident liability and any branches not included above. All companies must report on revenue received at the beginning of the premiums, additional premiums and loadings during January–June and July–December of each year; payment is made in the tax offices of the Secretary of the Treasury or in any credit institution.

Taxes and Loadings over Benefits. The tax on annual net profits is calculated on the balance sheets sent to the Secretary of the Treasury for approval once deductions for direct fines have been made or at the establishment of funds or reserves for fines, for fluctuations, or other provision which may be established by law or may be approved by the Secretary. Taxes payable by foreign companies on their capital is based on that which they have in their own country.

Other Taxes and Loadings. Budget costs for control and vigilance of insurance companies is divided among them as follows: 50% in proportion of the capital and reserves of each company; 30% in relation to premiums from policies issued in the previous year; 20% in relation to profits. National institutions which make no profits will pay a quota fixed by the Secretary of the Treasury. Quotas are payable monthly in advance to the Bank of Mexico.

Mortgage loans granted by insurance companies are taxed at a rate not exceeding 0.25%. Real estate property of insurance companies is taxed under the same conditions as any other obligated by this tax. Municipal taxes on the above real estate is under the same conditions as any other obligated by this tax.

VII. PRODUCTION (AGENTS)

Basic Legal Rules. These include the general law of insurance institutions of 31 August 1935 and the regulation for agents of insurance institutions of 29 September 1955.

Kinds of Agents. General trustees are authorized by contract to serve as agents and have powers to accept and change coverage. Trustees do not have these powers.

Previous Requirements. The agent should not previously have been disqualified. If a foreigner, he must prove his right to practice the profession in his native country. Aptitude tests are not required.

Authorization. The National Banking Commission on Insurance and Sureties, after approving the credentials of the agent, grants authorization at the request of the company hiring the agent. In life, accident, and illness branches, the agent will be authorized to operate with only one company. The length of authorization is subject to the duration of the contract of the agency.

Bail. An agent must convince the contracting company that he is capable to perform his duties. A specific sum of money is not fixed as guarantee.

Agency Contract. The contract is a mandate and must contain as basic points the duration, authority, branches and zones of operation, statute of retributions, and guarantees.

Retribution (Commissions). Commissions are determined by the agency contract but must not exceed the maximum set for each branch by the National Banking Commission on Insurance and Surety. Typical commissions are fire, 15–25%; third party, 10–20%; maritime and transport, 10–20%; other, 12.5–20%. Commissions may not be totally or partially conceded.

Official Protection. The Mexican Institution of Technical Agents of Insurance and Surety is a private association and membership is not compulsory.

The following persons are prohibited from dealing in insurance: officers and employees of the federal, state, and local government; of institutions of credit, sureties, insurance; insurance adjusters, and all persons who could, in the opinion of the National Banking Commission on Insurance and Surety, be prejudiced in the writing of insurance or represent a menace to the public or to insuring companies.

An agent's portfolio rights for life insurance will be respected throughout the time the contracts he made are in force. In damage insurance, the commissions for a new contract with a company already holding policies with the company go to the agent who obtained the first policies unless he has left the business or the insured requests in writing the nonintervention of such an agent.

In addition to civil and criminal liabilities for illegal operation, agents can be sanctioned with fines up to 5000 pesos ($400) imposed by the Secretary of the Treasury at the request of the National Banking Commission on Insurance and Surety.

VIII. INSTITUTIONAL BODIES

Governmental Groups. The Secretary of the Treasury and Public Credit is the controlling organization of insurance companies. It applies all legalities dealing with insurance.

The National Banking Commission on Insurance and Surety is the organization delegated by the Secretary of the Treasury for control and vigilance of insurance companies. It has a permanent committee with executive powers and a consultative committee. To be valid, its resolutions must be approved by the Secretary of the Treasury. Its basic powers are to exercise the vigilance which is set forth in the General Law on Insurance Institutions; approve rates of premiums, policies, and insurance contracts; resolve complaints against insurance companies; intervene in cases of disolution, liquidation, bankruptcy, or suspension of payments by insurance companies; inform regarding establishment of new companies or branches, or in cases of revocation or suspension of activities; confirm the statute of investments; approve balances; propose sanctions; undertake studies recommended by the Secretary of the Treasury; advise on interpretation of legal texts related to insurance.

Aseguradora Mexicana S.A. is the National Institution if Insurance created in 1942, which covers risks of official organizations (see section III). Aseguradora Nacional Agrícola y Ganadera, S.A. was created in 1961 to cover agricultural and livestock insurance (see section III). Compañía Mexicana de Seguros de Créditos S.A. is a private company organized in 1970 to support Mexican export programs with export credit for commercial risks. Aseguradora Hidalgo, S.A. is a decentralized institution which covers life insurance of government workers.

Associations. The Asociación Mexicana de Instituciones de Seguros promotes the insurance profession in Mexico, coordinating activities of companies in technical, political, and social aspects. Asociación Mexicana de Agentes Técnicos de Seguros y Fianzas assists professional formation of its agents in the technical aspects and in relations with insurance companies and the state. The Instituto Mexicano de Actuarios unites actuaries of insurance companies, coordinating and maintaining their professional work in accordance with the technological developments in insurance. The Oficina de Impedimentos has been created by life insurance companies for the control of unusual risks and rejections.

IX. CHARACTERISTICS OF THE SIXTIES

Compulsory Agricultural and Livestock Insurance. In 1962 the Aseguradora Nacional Agrícola y Ganadera, S.A. began operations. The law states that national credit institutions cannot grant credits without first soliciting agricultural and live stock insurance for agricultural or livestock exploitations to which credit is destined. Also, the state government, through the National Commission of Banking and Insurance insures that private credit institutions and auxiliary credit organizations contract this insurance under the same terms. By 1972 the company was to have extended operations to provide life insurance of 5,000 pesos to country workers.

New Rates for Insurance against Earthquake and Volcanic Eruptions.
These rates, which were effected in 1964, consider zone, type of construction, regularity, condition, and design. There is a compulsory franchise of 1% of the capital insured with a minimum of 2,500 and a maximum of 250,000 pesos. A change in rates is being studied.

Legal Modifications. In 1966 the General Law of Insurance Institution and the law regulating insurance contract (both of 1935) were reformed, authorizing installment premiums and automatic cancellation of insurance on nonpayment of premiums.

Labor Improvements. In 1969, by agreement of all companies, insurance employees fall under the Labor Regulation of Employees of Credit Institutions and Auxiliary Organizations, which provides larger economic and guarantee loans.

Restructure of Automobile Insurance. Because of problems facing this type of insurance, rates were restructured in 1969 to adapt them and to limit costs of acquiring this branch.

Constitution of the Compañía Mexicana de Créditos. In 1970 this company was created to cover commercial risks of foreign trading. Its organization was promoted by most insuring companies, and they contributed the necessary capital.

Merger of the National Commission of Insurance and the National Banking Commission. By decree of the executive power in late 1970, the National Commission of Banking and Insurance was created as the organization responsible for control and vigilance of banks and insurance institutions.

Insurance Development. Since 1960 the insurance business has increased at a higher annual rate than the national gross production. Large companies tend to rationalize their activities and have adopted modern techniques in electronic data processing; they have effected developmental plans for personnel and industrial relations; they have made important advances in updating coverage for industrial risks and in respective rates and regulations. Publicity campaigns have given consumers a favorable impression of insurance and have improved the image of the agent and the company.

X. FUNDAMENTAL LEGISLATION

Chronological Order

11 May 1933—Travel Insurance Bylaw.
31 August 1935—General Law of Insurance Institutions.
31 August 1935—Insurance Contract Regulating Law.
31 December 1947—Investment Regulating Law.
29 September 1955—Bylaw for Agents.
28 February 1956—National Banking Commission on Insurance and Surety Bylaw.

30 December 1961—Integral Agricultural and Live Stock Insurance Law.
7 July 1962—Group Insurance Bylaw.
6 September 1963—Integral Agricultural and Live Stock Insurance Bylaw.

By Subject

General Dispositions—General Law of Insurance Institutions, 31 August 1935.

Group Insurance—By law, 7 July 1962.

Insurance Contract—Regulating Law, 31 August 1935.

National Banking Commission on Insurance and Surety—Bylaw, 28 February, 1956.

Investments—Regulating Law, 31 December 1947.

Agents—Bylaw, 29 September 1955.

Travel Insurance—Bylaw, 11 May 1933.

Integral Agricultural and Life Stock—Law, 30 December 1961; Bylaw, 6 September 1963.

Paraguay

I. GENERAL INFORMATION

Historical Note. During the nineteenth century all insurance was provided by foreign companies, especially Argentinian companies and some European companies such as Royal Insurance. In 1904 the first regulating law covering insurance was passed. It was modified in 1905 and 1910 to facilitate and regulate foreign branch offices. In 1905 the first two national companies were established: La Paraguaya, S.A., which is still in operation, and La Nacional de Seguros. In 1947 decree-law No. 17,840 gave the Insurance Supervisory Office fiscal control of insurance companies.

Official Control. The Bank Supervisory Office is empowered to set rules and resolutions for the better operation of insurance companies. The Directorate of the Central Bank of Paraguay is authorized to enforce the rules in the decree-law of 10 February 1947.

Professional Statute. This is represented in the Insurance Company Association and in the Chamber of Motor Vehicle Insurers.

Market Structure. The market is composed of twenty-one companies; the seventeen national companies represent 83% of the premiums on the market; the four foreign companies provide the rest. Motor vehicle and fire insurance, representing approximately 70% of the market income, are the most important branches.

International Expansion. This is limited to three companies participating in the Latin American Reinsurance Pool, which has headquarters in Panama and accepts risks in that region.

Workmen's Compensation. This is required. Since 1950 it is incorporated into the Social Security law, and it is covered through the Institute of Social Provision.

Agents and Brokers. These persons are authorized by the Supervisory Office, which grants their licenses and records them in the Register after they have passed an examination. Only registered agents and brokers can conduct insurance activities.

Public Insurance. All public insurance is covered by Social Security.

Reinsurance. All reinsurance operations are conducted abroad.

II. FORM AND OPERATION OF PRIVATE INSURERS

Basic Legal Rules. Two laws govern insurance activities: the decree-law of 10 February 1947 and the Code of Commerce of 29 August 1891.

Legal Nature. In Paraguay insurance is conducted through joint stock companies. With foreign companies, any legal form accepted as valid in the country of origin is approved.

Social Purpose. This is limited to insurance operations and the administration of properties in which insurance companies have capital and reserves invested.

Operations Area. Operations are authorized for all branches of insurance provided minimum capital requirements are met.

Constitution Requirements. The minimum capital required for both national and foreign companies must be no less than 4,000,000 guaranies ($21,000) regardless of the branches of insurance sold. Minimums in each branch are fire, 2,500,000; motor vehicle, 1,000,000; merchandise, 1,000,000; life, 500,000; other risks, 200,000. If operations in life insurance are included, the minimum capital is 5,200,000 guaranies.

No definite ruling exists for warrant deposits for national or foreign companies. In both instances, the entire minimum capital must be disbursed.

Process of Authorization. Documentation for national and foreign companies is similar. National companies must present the following documents to the Supervisory Office: a copy of the decree granting them legal status; constitutional act and social statute act; details of shareholders, committee, manager and directors; insurance plans, policies, and rates. Life insurance companies must also present mortality tables, morbidity tables, exchange tables, and guaranteed securities tables. In addition to the above, foreign companies must present certification for operation in their home country and in foreign countries; the representative's powers; records, balances, and accounts for the past five years; and any other information requested.

Authorization procedure for both national and foreign companies includes formalization before the directorate of the Central Bank of Paraguay which, on the judgment of the Bank Supervisory Office, grants or denies authorization.

If legal requirements are met, authorization is automatic. When authorization is denied, an appeal can be made before the Directorate. If authorization is still denied, an appeal of administrative victimization may be made through legal channels. No official register of authorization exists, and authorizations do not have to be published.

Reporting Obligations. During the first twenty days of each month the company sends the Bank Supervisory Office a report of the previous month's operations. On 30 June and December 31 it submits a portfolio report and information on investments made from capital and reserves. During the ninety days following the end of the fiscal year (30 June) it submits to the Supervisory Office the annual balance, director's report according to the prescribed models, and profit and loss statement which must be published in one of the larger newspapers of the national capital. Foreign companies follow the same procedures and in addition they submit the director's report, balance, and profit and loss statement of the home office.

III. CONTRACTING

Basic Legal Rules. These include the Code of Commerce of 29 August 1891, and the decree-law on insurance legal statute of 10 February 1947.

Policies. Policies must be approved by the Supervisory Office before use in the market; approval of insurance propositions is not required, however. The law forsees the establishment of uniform policies to be issued by the Supervisory Office.

Rates. Rates are approved by the Supervisory Office after examining figures which determine the amount. Rates for fire, motor vehicle, and accidents of passengers insurance are compulsory. In the remaining branches they are uniform, being set by the Chamber of Insurers of the Argentinian Republic.

Required Insurances. Because of the risks involved, a compulsory insurance covers persons traveling from the national capital to the interior and vice versa. This was established by decree-law of 1 December 1958 and regulated in January 1959. No special ruling affects from which company insurance must be purchased—the insurer is free to elect all branches.

Foreign Insurance Restrictions. Covering risks with a foreign insurer abroad is prohibited except when authorized by the Supervisory Office. No company in Paraguay is willing to undertake this at present.

Companies operating in transport insurance may issue policies in foreign currency to cover import or export of merchandise if the insured or the beneficiary lives abroad and the payment of premiums is made in foreign or convertible currency.

IV. TECHNICAL RESERVES

Basic Legal Rules. These include the decree-law of 10 February 1947 and resolution of the Supervisory Office of 20 December 1955 and 19 June 1959.

Classes. Life classes are formed by the integral reserve, policy by policy, with no deductions whatever. Premium reserve is formed by 40% of the premiums of the fiscal year. In covering outstanding losses for life insurance, the amount will be equal to the total payable under conditions of the policy. For other branches, the total amount will be paid when confirmed by the assessor. In the event of no final settlement of the claim, half of the sum of the official assessment of both parties will be awarded, provided the assessment of the damage is not 60% of the sum claimed. There are no special regulations regarding deviations of loss ratio or fluctuation of values. For other reserves, the insurance companies must create a special reserve fund with a minimum of 10% of their annual net profits until reaching 50% of the guaranteed capital. To this reserve must be added profits from negotiation of properties constituting the reserve, even if the 50% sum has been reached. The purpose of this reserve is to meet devaluations of investments and extraordinary losses.

All technical and voluntary reserves may be invested in the following properties with the purpose of attaining the highest profits: public titles and titles guaranteed by Paraguay, mortgage notes and national pledges, mortgage loans on properties in Paraguay, properties in Paraguay, loans on policies, and other investments accepted by the Supervisory Office.

General Requirements of Goods To Be Used as Reserve Covers. Investment in real estate requires permission of the Supervisory Office. When investments are in the form of loans with property mortgage guarantees, the loan must not exceed 200,000 guaranies per beneficiary nor the fiscal value of the properties. The write-off terms are subject to the following limits: commercial, one year without option to extend; industrial, agricultural, and live stock, one year with option to extend one year more; construction of dwellings or refinancing of debts arising from these, three years with option to extend for two more years.

General Limits on Investment. On loans with property mortgage guarantee, investment may be made up to 40% of the total of reserves (to 50% if not operating in life insurance). Investments may cover up to 30% on construction of the company's own buildings or acquisition of buildings (50% if not operating in life insurance); or up to 30% on loans against policies.

V. REINSURANCE

Basic Legal Rule. This is the decree-law of 10 February 1947 on the Insurance Statute.

Present Statute. No legal statute regulates activities of reinsurers. Most surpluses are placed in foreign countries under authorization of the respective cessation contract by the Supervisory Office.

VI. TAXES

Basic Legal Rule. The decree-law No. 17840 of 10 February 1947 on insurance statute covers taxes.

Taxes and Loadings over Premiums. The insurance company pays the following taxes for each policy issued: Law 1003/64, stamp tax, 1% of the premium; Law 364/64, 5% of the premium, destined for the maintenance of the Central Railways of Paraguay; Law 11711, 50% of the premium, which substitutes income tax payable by the insured. Other charges which include bank costs and policy costs form another 4%, and 2% of the premiums (set by

Resolution 774/70 of the Bank Supervisory Office) maintains costs of this office. Total taxes and charges equal 13.5% of the premium.

Taxes and Loadings over Profits.   The Income Tax Law 9240/59 sets a tax of 25% on profits above G.100,000. Law 1171 also applies to insurance companies. Article 5 of this law presumes that insurance companies receive a taxable income of no less than 6% of the value of the net premiums from cancellations. Law 1003/64, stamp duty, imposes a 1% tax on net profits according to the balance sheet.

The following taxes also affect insurance operations: Law 70/68, 0.5% of integrated capital and accumulated reserves; a fiscal tax under law 344/71, 1% of assets smaller than G10,000,000 and G100,000 when assets are greater than G10,000,000.

VII. PRODUCTION (AGENTS)

Basic Legal Rules.   These include decree-law of 10 February 1947; resolutions of the Supervisory Office of 27 January 1959, 14 September 1960, 2 January 1961, 23 January 1961, and 20 March 1961.

Kinds of Agents.   Classifications do not exist. All agents are mediators in insurance activities.

Previous Requirements.   The agent must present the following documents to the Supervisory Office: certificate of good conduct, health record book, driver's license, certificate of approval of the insurance company for which he works. He must also pass an aptitude test for each branch of insurance conducted by the Supervisory Office.

Authorization.   The Supervisory Office grants the insurance agent a license which is valid for a year and renewable for periods of one year provided the agent sells at least twelve policies during the previous period and his company is agreeable to the renewal. Licenses are registered in the Insurance Agent Register kept by the General Comptroller of Insurances.

Bail.   Bail is not subject to regulation.

Agency Contract.   This is not subject to regulation.

Commissions.   Commissions are set by the insurance company except for the maximum in the following branches: fire, 20%; motor vehicle, 20%; plate glass, 20%; transport, 10%; life stock, 12%.

Official Protection.   This is not subject to regulation.

VIII. INSTITUTIONAL BODIES

Governmental Entities.   The Bank Supervisory Office is dependent on the Central Bank, an autonomous state organization, which regulates fiscal responsibilities of insurance companies, their operations, and everything related to the financial statute, plans, rates, contract conditions, accounting, functions of directors, agents, and publicity.

The directorate of the Central Bank of Paraguay is an organization that, since 1952, replaces the Monetary Board and which has power to set rules and bylaws of the decree-law of 10 February 1947.

Associations. The Insurance Companies Association is a trade union which defends and coordinates the interests of affiliated companies before the public authorities. It also provides technical and statistical studies of Paraguyan insurance. The Chamber of Motor Vehicle Insurers is a technical commission for studies and assessments. It is comprised of one representative from each of the associated companies. Other organizations include the Insurance Producers Association and the Insurance Employees Association, which cooperate for the defense and representation of their affiliates.

IX. CHARACTERISTICS OF THE SIXTIES

Constitution of the Paraguayan Insurance Companies Association. This institution, organized on 28 May 1963, united Paraguayan insurance companies. Its objects are to promote harmonious development on insurance activities, help create conditions suitable for the private insurer to realize his maximum goals, tighten the bonds between insurers, contribute to the economic development of the country within the bounds of a free economy, and any other object complimentary to the above.

Proliferation of Companies. Only eleven companies operated in Paraguay before 1960. Since then ten more have been organized.

Market Expansion. In 1960 premiums totaled G73,278,970 ($383,300). In 1970 the increment was 796.9% (G546,217,200 or $2,951,289). Thus, insurance activities have increased and made an important contribution to the national economy in this decade. Nevertheless, many companies have shown reduced profits and some have registered losses.

Compulsory Insurance for Passenger Accidents. In November 1962 a new national law regulates compulsory insurance against accidents to passengers. This ammended the decree-law 180 of 1 December 1958 covering the same subject.

Increase in Motor Vehicle Rates. A 15% increase in motor vehicle rates was established by resolution No. 1 of 28 July 1967 of the Bank Supervisory Office.

X. FUNDAMENTAL LEGISLATION

Chronological Order

10 February 1947–decree-law on Insurance Statute (No. 17840).

20 December 1955–resolution of the Bank Supervisory Office on investment of reserves.

2 August 1957–resolution of the directorate of the Central Bank on fire insurance rates.

26 December 1957—resolution of the directorate of the Central Bank on minimum capital.

11 June 1958—resolution of the directorate of the Central Bank on minimum capital.

27 January 1959—resolution of the Supervisory Office on commissions.

29 April 1959—resolution of the Central Bank (directorate) on the rates of motor vehicle insurance.

19 April 1959—resolution of the Bank Supervisory Office on investment of reserves.

28 September 1959—resolution of the directorate of the Central Bank on the rates of accident insurance.

14 September 1960—resolution of the Supervisory Office on agents.

21 September 1960—resolution of the directorate of the Central Bank on transports (foreign currency).

2 January 1961—resolution of the Supervisory Office on agents.

23 January 1961—resolution of the Supervisory Office on agents.

20 May 1961—resolution of the Supervisory Office on commissions.

By Subject

General dispositions—decree-law on the insurance statute, 10 February 1947.

Minimum capital—resolution of the directorate of the Central Bank, 26 December 1957; resolution of the directorate of the Central Bank, 11 June 1958.

Rates—Fire, resolution of the directorate of the Central Bank, 2 August 1957; motor vehicle, resolution of the directorate of the Central Bank, 29 April 1959; accident, resolution of the directorate of the Central Bank, 28 September 1959.

Foreign currency—transport, resolution of the directorate of the Central Bank, 21 September 1960.

Investment of reserves—resolutions of the Bank Supervisory Office, 20 December 1955 and 19 June 1959.

Commissions—resolutions of the Supervisory Office, 27 January 1959, and 20 May 1961.

Agents—resolutions of the Supervisory Office of 14 September 1960, 2 January 1961, and 23 January 1961.

Peru

I. GENERAL INFORMATION

Historical Note. Insurance companies began operating in Peru in the late nineteenth century—especially the Compañía Chilena de Seguros of Chile and the Sudamericana of Brazil. Before this time agents of English companies also had been active. The first Peruvian insurance company, the Compañía Internacional de Seguros de Perú, was established in 1895. In that same year a law on the establishment of insurance companies was passed, and in 1897 a decree was set that led to the organization of the Fiscal Inspection Office, a forerunner of the Bank and Insurance Supervisory Office.

Official Control. The Bank and Insurance Supervisory Office, organized in 1937 to supersede the Fiscal Inspection Office, regulates insurance activities in Peru. This office is under the Ministry of the Treasury.

Professional Statute. The Peruvian Insurers Association is the only organization representing insurance companies. From a corporate point of view this association defends and represents its members before public authorities and aids its associates by providing information and technical assistance.

Market Structure. By the end of 1970 twenty companies, including one Brazilian company, comprised the market. The three largest companies receive more than 30% of the total market. Fire, life, and motor vehicle insurance are the most important, representing 18%, 16%, and 15% for the total market respectively.

International Expansion. Lacks development.

Workmen's Compensation. This insurance is compulsory; it is provided by private companies through the Social Security of the nation.

Agents and Brokers. No special aspects need discussing.

Public Insurance. The National Bank regulates insurance covering risks on state property.

Reinsurance. Reinsurance is not professionally developed. The decree-law of 16 September 1971 grants authority to the National Bank to provide foreign and national reinsurance.

II. FORM AND OPERATION OF PRIVATE INSURERS

Basic Legal Rules. These include law of 21 December 1895 on organization of insurance companies, extended by Supreme Decrees of 9 June 1943 and 28 November 1958; and the Supreme Decree of 9 June 1943 and the law of 20 June 1952 on insurance company capital.

Legal Nature. Stock companies.

Social Purpose. Companies are limited exclusively to insurance operations.

Operations Area. A company may operate in all forms of insurance authorized by the Supervisory Office provided legal constitutional requirements are met.

Constitution Requirements. Minimum stock for national and foreign companies is 5,000,000 gold soles ($57,000) disbursed and invested in equal parts in real estate properties in Peru and in national securities quoted on the stock market. The shares representative of the capital belong primarily to Peruvian shareholders.

Warrant deposit technically does not exist, but a reserve fund is required of both national and foreign companies to guarantee insurers (see section IV).

Process of Authorization. Documentation for national companies includes filing an application with the Supervisory Office, accompanied by the articles of the association, technical basis and projects of policies, details of branch operation, projects and reports of reinsurance contracts when they are with foreign companies, and receipt of the guarantee capital deposited with the Deposits and Consignations Fund. In addition to the above, foreign companies must show proof of power of attorney for persons representing them in Peru.

After both foreign and national companies apply, the Supervisory Office publishes the application in up to three periodicals: the one charged with publishing official announcements, one in the Peruvian capital, and, if the company plans to establish its headquarters outside Lima, in a large-circulation journal in the place of establishment. After authorization has been granted by the Supervisory Office, the Executive Power decides, with aid of a Supreme Resolution issued by the Ministry of the Treasury and Commerce, on final authorization. A company, being denied authorization by the Supervisory Office, can appeal to the Executive Power. Authorization provides for a company being listed in the Public Register controlled by the Code of Commerce.

Reporting Obligations. Both foreign and national companies must publish the balance sheet and profits and losses in the newspaper *El Peruano* and in the primary newspaper which have a legal section in regional capitals. Each July and January they must give the Supervisory Office a sworn statement of contracts negotiated during the past six months, their value, corresponding premiums, and other details requested by the administration. Companies must provide the Bank and Insurance Supervisory Office with all information it requests for compilation of the general market statistics.

III. CONTRACTING

Basic Legal Rules. These include the law of 27 January 1943 and the regulation of 9 June 1943, Law 4916 and the regulation on life insurance of the employee, the law of 25 October 1966 and the decree of 11 May 1967 on decreasing mortgage duty on decreasing term life insurance, and the Supreme Resolution of 31 March 1958 on accidents at work.

Policies. All policies are of uniform design, and they are supplied by the Peruvian Insurers Association. They may be changed only by the government at the request of the PIA.

Rates. Rates also are uniform. They have been set by the PIA and may be approved or changed by the Ministry of the Treasury at the request of the Association through the Supervisory Office.

Compulsory Insurance. Employers in commerce must provide life insurance for all employees who have four years of uninterrupted service. The amount of coverage initially equals one-third of the total amount earned during the four-year period and is updated each four years in this same proportion.

All persons taking a mortgage loan for the construction, acquisition, enlargement, or reconstruction of their "domicile" must take out a decreasing mortgage duty life insurance in favor on the borrower and in benefit of his heirs or third parties. This insurance is exempt from all taxes.

Workmen's compensation must be provided by contractors and subcontractors for all construction workers before they begin working.

All life insurance must be purchased through national companies; foreign companies are expressly excluded.

Foreign Insurance Restrictions. See section VI. Limitations include taxes and assured capitals placed on operations outside Peru that could have been kept inside the country.

IV. TECHNICAL RESERVES

Basic Legal Rules. These include the law of 21 November 1928, the Supreme Resolution of 7 March 1929, and the Supreme Decree of 25 September 1934 on investment of reserves.

Classes. No concrete rules exist on mathematical and other technical reserves. The usual rules are applied on their constitution. For other reserves, a reserve fund must be formed with 20% of the annual profits and up to a total established by law. Once the total has been attained, the application continues indefinitely with increments of no less than 5% of the profits from each fiscal year.

All technical reserves on policies issued in Peru must be invested in Peru. Investments may be made in properties; titles, or shares of public credit, municipal shares, or shares in nationally guaranteed institutions; loans in cash on life insurance policies or on guaranteed mortgages on properties.

General Requirements of Goods To Be Used as Reserve in Covers. Real estate property must be located in Peru. Titles or shares in private institutions must be recorded in the Mercantile Register and be quoted on the Lima Stock

Market. Titles or securities can be substituted with others that have equal or higher quotation on the Stock Market. Properties or mortgages may be substituted only when they are exchanged for those of a higher guarantee.

V. REINSURANCE

Basic Legal Rules. These include the law of 21 December 1895 on the establishment of insurance companies. It was extended by Supreme Decrees of 9 June 1943 and 28 November 1958. Also the decree-law of 16 September 1971 concedes to the National Bank the monopoly of reinsurance activity of exterior operations.

Legal Nature. Stock companies.

Process of Authorization. National and foreign companies authorized to operate in direct insurance are automatically authorized to operate in reinsurance.

Reporting Obligations. These are similar to those for companies operating only in direct insurance.

Balances and Remittances in Foreign Currency. Although no limitation exists technically, as a rule operations in foreign currency must be converted to Peruvian money at the exchange rate at that moment.

Other Aspects. Until recently there was considerable liberty in the interchange of reinsurance business, both with Peruvian companies, where there was complete freedom, and with foreign companies, who were limited only in that they had to have minimum guarantee capitals and mimimum reserves, they had to belong to the insurance associations of their home country, and they had to have permission of the Supervisory Office. A radical change, however, was effected by the decree-law of 16 September 1971, which grants the National Bank the exclusive authority to deal in reinsurance in and from foreign countries. Changes include the following: (1) The National Bank is the only entity authorized to operate in or from foreign countries. This right is exclusive. (2) Contracts of reinsurance arranged with companies abroad were cancelled on 31 December 1971. Acceptations and optional concessions were annulled on their next expiratory date without option of extension. (3) Companies established in Peru will place excesses of their net self-retention on the national market, including the National Bank. (4) Acceptation of the National Bank regarding national and foreign business will be ceded or re-ceded in the national market or abroad. (5) The National Bank is authorized to adopt the measures it considers most convenient for carrying out these rulings.

VI. TAXES

Basic Legal Rules. These include the law of 28 April 1933, the law of 6 July 1939, the law of 27 January 1943 and the bylaw of 16 October 1943, the law of 2 December 1954, the Supreme Decree of 31 October 1955, the law of 14 May 1965, and the regulatory decree of 2 November 1965.

Taxes and Loadings over Premiums. A 5% tax is levied on the value of premiums on insurance and reinsurance contracted in foreign insurance companies. A 5% tax is levied on the value of fire insurance premiums contracted directly by individuals with foreign companies. A .25% tax is levied on assured capital regarding insurance contracts with companies not established in Peru. Exempt from these taxes are: (1) capitals for risks not covered by national companies, (2) capital for risks covered by national companies which exceed the maximum covered and reinsured by those in Peru, (3) capital for risks when national companies do not insure an entire object, (4) capital for inseparable risks when national companies insure only one or some of such risks, (5) capital for risks that national companies do not insure except when combined with others that the client does not wish to insure, (6) capital for risks that national companies do not wish to cover, (7) capital for risks of exportation or importation including transport, and (8) reinsured capital.

A tax of 2.50% is levied on premiums of all fire insurance contracted in Peru; this tax maintains firemen's services and is paid by the insurer and does not alter the amount of the premium. A tax of 35% is levied on the value of the premiums of direct insurances placed abroad. This tax is paid by the insured.

Other taxes include (1) receipts and accounts for payment of insurance effected in Peru or abroad is taxed at a rate of 5% except for life insurance which is taxed at 1%. (2) Receipts for amounts paid by insurers in respect of claims and settlements are taxed at a rate of 3% except for life insurance where the rate is 1%. (3) A 3% tax is imposed on the balance of accounts in reinsurance. (4) A six-month quota to subsidize Supervisory Office expenses is equivalent to 3% of the paid premiums for each insuring company.

Taxes and Loadings over Profits. A 5% tax is levied on the net annual profits of fire insurance companies and on the departments of fire insurance of the general insurance companies established in Peru.

VII. INSTITUTIONAL BODIES

Governmental Bodies. The Bank and Insurance Supervisory Office is the official body under the Ministry of the Treasury, which regulates Peruvian insurance companies to see that they observe the laws and dispositions. The Office was established by Supreme Decree of 24 November 1937, ratified by the law of 15 December 1938, and replaces the Fiscal Inspection Office of Insurance Companies established in June 1897. The Contributions Supervisory, also under the Ministry of the Treasury, regulates fiscal control of insurance companies. The National Bank is the public body which, by decree-law of 16 September 1971, controls the monopoly of reinsurance activity in and from foreign countries.

Associations. ADPA, the Peruvian Insurers Association, is a private body representing insurance companies in Peru. This group helps unify and coordinate companies in the market through standardization of policies, rates, and production commissions. It also helps develop insurance activities; promote technical, contractual, and company organization aspects; represent and defend its associates before public authorities.

EDCES, the Insurance Training School, was created in 1969 by the Peruvian Insurers Association to train technical and professional insurance employees. It is financed by the insurance companies.

VIII. CHARACTERISTICS OF THE SIXTIES

In 1965 by Law 15.564 a special tax affects insurances effected abroad. In the same year, by Supreme Decree 182–H, the system of paying insurance premiums is regulated coordinately.

In 1966 Law 16.268 decreases mortgage duty on decreasing term life insurance, regulated by decree of 11 May 1967.

In 1969 the Insurance Training School, financed by the Peruvian Insurers Association, is founded.

In 1971 by decree-law of 16 September, the National Bank is granted authority to act exclusively in reinsurance operations with foreign companies.

IX. FUNDAMENTAL LEGISLATION

Chronological Order

21 December 1895—Law regulating insurance company establishment.

23 June 1897—Supreme Decree controlling insurance companies.

21 November 1928—Law 6331 regulating insurance company reserves.

7 March 1929—Supreme Resolution regulating insurance company reserves.

28 April 1933—Law 7.750 on the system of taxation of insurance companies.

25 September 1934—Supreme Decree regulates reserves of insurance companies.

18 November 1935—Supreme Resolution on insurance statistics.

24 November 1937—Supreme Decree controlling insurance companies and capitalization companies.

15 December 1938—Law 8793 controlling insurance companies and capitalization companies.

6 July 1939—Law 8914 regulating the taxing of insurance companies and of fire insurance.

27 January 1943—Law 9796 regulating the taxing of insurance companies, fire insurance, and insurance premiums.

9 June 1943—Supreme Decree governing insurance companies.

20 June 1952—Law 11850 regulating insurance companies.

2 December 1954—Law 8914 regulating the taxing of insurance companies and of fire insurance.

31 October 1955—Supreme Decree regulating the taxing of insurance companies.

31 March 1958—Supreme Resolution 30 on the policies of insurance against accidents at work and contractors.

28 November 1958—Supreme Decree 20 on establishment of insurance companies.

14 May 1965—Law 15564 regulating tax on insurance effected outside Peru and the "stamp duty" tax.

11 May 1967—Decree regulating the decreasing mortgage duty on decreasing term life insurance.

16 September 1971—Regulating Decree on the activities of the National Bank.

By Subject

Insurance Company Capital—Regulating Law, 27 January 1943; Supreme Decree, 9 June 1943; Regulating Law, 20 June 1952.

Controlling insurance companies—Supreme Decree, 23 June 1897; idem and capitalization companies, 24 November 1937; idem, 15 December 1938.

Establishment of insurance companies—Regulating Law, 21 December 1895; Supreme Decree, 9 June 1943; idem, 28 November 1958.

Insurance statistics—Supreme Resolution, 18 November 1935.

Taxes—law regulating tax on insurances effected outside Peru and the "stamp duty" tax, 14 May 1965.

Policies of insurance against accidents at work and the contractors—Supreme Resolution, 31 May 1958.

Insurance Premiums—Regulating Law, 21 January 1943; Supreme Decree, 9 June 1943.

Reinsurance—Decree-law regulating activities of the National Bank, 16 September 1971.

Insurance Company Reserves—Regulating law, 21 November 1928; Supreme Resolution, 7 March 1929; Supreme Decree, 25 September 1934.

Decreasing Mortgage Duty on decreasing term life insurance—regulating decree, 11 May 1967.

Taxation—law regulating taxation of insurance companies and fire insurance, 6 July 1939; law, 2 December 1954; Supreme Decree, 31 October 1955; law, 28 April 1933; law, 27 January 1943; regulation of taxation of insurance and of insurance companies, 27 January 1943.

Portugal

I. GENERAL INFORMATION

Historical Note. King D. Diniz granted an ordinance in May 1293 permitting the creation of the Portuguese Merchants Society by which merchants could protect themselves from emergencies from foreign commerce. In the fourteenth century a royal ordinance ruled that Portuguese merchants owning vessels of more than fifty tons were required to join a mutual company to indemnify marine losses. This was the origin of the Companhia das Naos which is now under government control. In 1592 an antecedent of the marine insurance law appeared in Venice—the Tractatus de Assecurationibus Mercatorum—written by Pedro de Samtem, a Portuguese citizen. In the nineteenth century, trade union assistance associations permitting indemnities or subsidies in the event of accident or illness to their associates, were formed. The first Portuguese insurance company, Bonaça, was founded in 1808. In 1907 the first decree regarding the activities and financial control of insurance companies was published. This constitutes the basic legislation still in force in Portugal.

Official Control. The Insurance Inspection Board of the Ministry of Finance has responsibility for supervision of insurance activities. This board was established by a decree of 5 November 1929 to replace the former National Insurance Board. By decree of 12 April 1971 the National Insurance Board was reestablished in an advisory capacity.

Professional Statute. The laws cover three organizations: (1) Credit and Insurance Corporation, which integrates employers and workers in the credit and insurance business; (2) the Underwriters Association, a cooperative organization representing national and foreign insurance companies; (3) the National Syndicates of Insurance Professionals, an association of employees of the Lisbon and Oporto districts. There are no professional organizations for insurance agents.

Market Structure. The thirty-nine national insurance companies account for 87% of the total market. The remaining 38 are foreign companies. Three companies sell nearly a third of all insurance. Only five national companies operate exclusively in reinsurance. Motor vehicle insurance is the most important, representing 28% of the market. Workmen's compensation is next with 24%, and life insurance is third with 15%.

International Expansion. Portuguese companies conduct activities in metropolitan areas and in overseas provinces. Only one national company operates in other European countries.

Workmen's Compensation. Various social security banks cover most of the Portuguest population against illness, accident, and death. Companies are required to transfer responsibility for occupational accidents to insurance companies unless they are economically capable of covering such risks themselves.

Agents and Brokers. No specific law regulates insurance agents and brokers. A new law of 12 April 1971, however, states that intermediaries are subject to rules, considering their categories, limiting the lines in which they can operate, and therefore limiting their rights and responsibilities. Intermediaries have no restrictions, and they may work simultaneously with different companies. Because of keen competition between companies and the fact that agents can work with different companies has caused an abnormal increase in commissions received by intermediaries.

Public Insurance. In addition to compulsory insurance on accidents, illnesses and death covered by the Social Security Bank and workmen's compensation insurance covered by the insurance companies, credit insurance, sold exclusively by the Credit Insurance Company, also is required.

Reinsurance. Most reinsurance is placed with foreign groups, especially through the London market. It is underdeveloped locally.

II. FORM AND OPERATION OF PRIVATE INSURERS

Basic Legal Rules. The decree of 21 October 1929 covers operation and supervision of the insurance industry. The decree of 5 November 1929 complements the earlier decree. This decree also creates the Insurance Inspection Board and the decree of 13 December 1932 regulates insurance inspection. The decree-law of 3 March 1936 regulates the operation of the Underwriters Association. The law of 12 April 1971 establishes a new system of insurance and reinsurance activities, but its regulation is pending.

Legal Nature. Joint stock companies or mutual societies.

Social Purpose. This is limited exclusively to insurance and reinsurance.

Constitutional Requirements. By decree of 5 November 1929 the minimum capital required for national joint stock companies is 1,500,000 Escudos ($54,000) if operating in life or personal accident insurances, 1,000,000 escudos if working only in lines, and 2,500,000 if dealing in all lines. The law of 12 April 1971 provides for a minimum of 30,000,000 Escudos ($1,070,000). The only requirement for foreign companies is that they maintain in their home countries the minimum capital required of national companies in Portugal.

National and foreign companies must put up a warrant deposit of 500,000 Escudos if they sell life insurance, 30,000 if they sell workmen's compensation, and 250,000 if they sell other lines. These deposits are to be in cash or public state values (treasury bonds or titles of public debts). Companies selling more than one line of insurance must deposit funds to cover all lines with which they deal. Mutual companies must pay minor deposits which, except for occupational hazards, cover reserves.

Process of Authorization. Documentation for national companies includes deeds of constitution, laws, guarantee deposit certificates, and a certificate that the company name or policy names are not identical to those of any other existing company. In addition life insurance companies must present technical bases on mortality table; differences between risk premium and gross premium assigned for administration expenses, calculation formulas for premiums; mathematical reserves, reduction and surrended values; company condition for reinsurance acceptance; policy forms and premium rates. The same holds for foreign companies. In addition they must present a transaction certificate from the home country which states which lines they are authorized to sell. Foreign companies also must appoint a legal representative to carry out official duties.

Authorization for both national and foreign companies is granted by the Minister of Finance on approval of general credit and insurance inspection. He shall approve or reject authorization on the basis of public interest. This approval or rejection must be documented and be published in the government gazette within ninety days. Authorization must be recorded in the Register of Insurance Companies.

Reporting Obligations. Foreign and national companies must submit a financial report to the Insurance Inspection Board before March 31 each year. This report includes balance, profits, losses, portfolio of values, and buildings, report on commercial and economic status of the company. In addition foreign companies must present a report of operations of the head office.

III. CONTRACTING

Basic Legal Rules. These include the Commercial Code of 28 June 1888, the decree of 21 October 1907 on operation and supervision of the insurance industry, the decree of 5 November 1929 which complements the 1907 decree, the law of 12 April 1971 which regulates insurance activities.

Policies. The permanent commissions of insurance underwriters prepare uniform policies for motor and workmen's compensation insurances, subject to the approval of the Minister of Finance. Policies for other lines are prepared by the company and require approval of the Minister of Finance.

Rates. Rates are uniform for motor, workmen's compensation, fire, and personal accident insurance. Although rates for other lines are unrestricted, they are subject to being brought to uniformity by the Minister of Finance after he receives the report of insurance inspection authorities.

Compulsory Insurance. Three types of risks must be covered in Portugal: (1) Insurance for employees of industry and commerce covers old age, invalidity, death, disease, maternity, and occupational diseases. Civil employees and military servicemen are covered by a special system. (2) Workmen's compensation—all industries with more than five permanent employees who are not financially able to provide the above insurance are covered by workmen's compensation through private insurance companies. (3) Collective transport insurance is required for any company providing public collective transport. The binder is 10,000 escudos per passenger or 10 escudos per kilogram load.

Insurance for industry and commerce is the concern of the Social Security Bank, labor unions, cooperatives, and pension and social security institutions. Credit insurance is provided exclusively by the Credit Insurance Society, a quasigovernmental company.

Foreign Insurance Restrictions. Contracts underwritten by insurance companies not authorized to operate in Portugal shall not be recognized as valid (decree-law of 27 July 1940). National and foreign companies are exempted from this ruling when they refuse to accept the coverage of risks or in doing so charge an excessive rate. Under those conditions the insurance may be placed abroad with prior authorization of the General Credit and Insurance Inspection Board.

IV. TECHNICAL RESERVES

Basic Legal Rules. These include the decree of 21 October 1907 on activities and supervision of the insurance industry, the decree of 5 November 1929 complementing this decree, the decree of 5 November 1907, and the decree of 9 August 1934.

Classes. Mathematical (Life) must be calculated in accordance with technical notes submitted by each company for approval of the Insurance Inspection Board.

Premium Reserve is called "Guarantee Reserve." It is equivalent to 33% of collected premiums including surcharges. Except in insurance coverage for less than one year (agriculture and merchandise risks, for example) the reserve is 10%.

Outstanding losses includes the total amount for losses, due capital, income or profits of insured persons pending payment at the end of each fiscal year which are considered to remain pending till June 30 of the following fiscal year. Global calculation systems or written premiums are not admitted.

Fluctuation of values must be constituted should there be a debit balance between real value and purchase value of chattel or real estate titles.

Investment on income exceeding guarantee deposit must be made in public debt titles, obligations of Portuguese General Company of Predial Credit and of Municipal Chambers, obligations or credit titles of any type with state guarantee, loans on life insurance policies issued by own company, real estate, or mortgage loans on real estate.

General Requirements of Goods To Be Used as Reserve Coverage. Private values, national or foreign, must be authorized by the Ministry of Finance. Real estate must be on the Continent or adjacent islands or in overseas Portuguese territory.

General Limits of Investment. Limits on technical reserves include 100% on public debt titles, losses on policies, and mortgage loans on urban real estate; 50% on obligations of the General Company of Portuguese Predial Credit or of municipal chambers, or on purcase of real estate; up to 30% on private values of any type.

Limits on mathematical reserves, in addition to investments appropriate to cover any class of technical reserve (providing the amount does not exceed the guarantee deposit), 100% on loans of life insurance policies issued by the company; up to 50% on urban real estate. In addition to investments capable of covering any class of technical reserve, the amount not exceeding the guarantee deposit may be invested in urban real estate, up to 80% in case of current risks, or up to 20% in case of outstanding loss reserves.

V. REINSURANCE

Basic Legal Rules. These include the decree of 21 October 1907 on operation and control of the insurance industry, the decree of 5 November 1929 complementing the earlier decree, and the law of 12 April 1971 regulating insurance activity.

Legal Nature. Joint stock companies. Mutual companies cannot accept reinsurance.

Process of Authorization. It is similar to that established for a company operating in direct insurance. Joint stock companies operating in reinsurance must indicate this fact in the title of constitution. Foreign companies authorized to sell direct insurance may accept reinsurance. To operate exclusively in reinsurance it is not necessary to establish a branch of the company in Portugal.

Reporting Obligations. These are similar to those for direct insurance.

Balances and Remittances in Foreign Currency. Although there is no special ruling in this matter, all exchange operations are authorized by the Bank of Portugal.

Official Control. This is similar to that established for direct insurance. It is limited for national companies operating solely in reinsurance and nonexistent for foreign companies with no branches in Portugal.

VI. TAXES

Basic Legal Rules. These include the decree of 21 October 1907 on activities and supervision of insurance, the law of 26 March 1923 on surcharge for fire services, the decree of 28 November 32 (modified by decree-laws of 24 November 1947 and 5 April 1968) on stamp tax, the decree-law of 31 March 1936 on surcharge; the decree-law of 10 September 1962 on tax on capital; and the decree-law of 1 July 1963 on industrial contribution.

Taxes and Charges over Premiums. All companies are subject to a 1% tax on collected premiums and a contribution (policy seal) on insurance policies, premiums, policy cost, and any additional amounts included in the premium—2% on life and occupational, 3% on marine and inland transport, and 5% in other lines. These taxes may be indirectly charged to the insured persons.

Nonfiscal surcharges include the tax collected for insurance inspection—2.5% drawn on total direct insurance premiums written by the companies (national and foreign companies operating only in reinsurance are exempted); for insurance companies—1.5% estimated surcharge on total direct insurances collected (companies must pay a minimum of 1,200 escudos annually); for fire services—equivalent to 6% on fire and 2% on agriculture insurances (national and foreign companies operating exclusively in reinsurance are exempted).

Taxes and Charges on Profits. A tax is imposed on profits obtained through commercial or industrial operations. Usually this tax is applicable to profits obtained in Portugal (not the colonies). This tax consists of three categories of contributors—large enterprises, medium enterprises, and small enterprises. Joint stock insurance companies pay a tax under the large enterprises group at the rate of 18%.

VII. PRODUCTION (AGENTS)

Basic Legal Rules. None apply to this sector.

Kinds of Agents. The professional agent does not exist in a separate or legal form. In practice three categories with distinct functions exist—agents, correspondents, and representatives; subagents, brokers, and company employees; and insurance companies acting as insurance brokers.

Previous Requirements. An agent must be at least eighteen years old and in possession of civil and political rights. Foreigners can be agents, also.

Authorization. None is required because of the unrestricted nature of the agent.

Bail. Not required although some companies require a bail insurance.

Agency Contracts. These are commercial and the content is not regulated.

Commissions. Although no uniform regulation exists, the normal commission percentages include automobile, 12.5%; occupational 5%; marine 10%; and fire, causalty, and general lines 20%. Commissions from life insurance vary according to the insurance period. For instance, in a twenty-year insurance, the commission is 60% plus 10,000 escudos for each 1,000,000 escudos of capital insured.

Official Protection. A professional association or unions to arbitrate with the companies are nonexistent, and there is no provision for social security protection on agents. No general regulation covers renewal rights, but individual companies establish the agents' rights.

VIII. INSTITUTIONAL BODIES

Government Entities. The Ministry of Finance is in charge of supervising insurance company operations and controlling fulfillment of insurance legislation. This supervision is carried out by insurance inspectors. Inspection includes credit inspection as well as general inspection of credit and insurance.

The National Insurance Board is the consulting body on insurance policy of the Ministries of Finance and Foreign Affairs. The Minister of Finance directs activities. The Board studies and makes proposals on minimum requirements of company solvency, attempts to decrease risks and prevent loss, and any other aspect for improving the structure and function of the insurance market. A law of 12 April 1971 with no regulation to date created and regulates this Board.

The Credit Insurance Company is a pro-government joint stock company created by decree-law of 3 April 1969. It supervises coverage of export commercial credits and internal credits as well as coverage procedure for the state on political and extraordinary risks deriving from export credits.

Associations. The Underwriters Association is formed by national and foreign insurance companies or companies planning to sell insurance. The association protects insurance companies' interests as well as insurance matters of public interest before the state and other corporations. It fixes minimum rates for different lines, elaborates on statistics, provides information, and assures the liberty of concurrence between companies.

The Employees Trade Union is a public organization formed by insurance company employees. It represents and protects interests of its associates.

The Credit and Insurance Corporation is a public organization grouping all Portuguese corporations and representing both employers and workmen in credit and insurance activities. A cooperative organization, it is in charge of studies on technical problems, organization of congresses, etc. It is divided into a credit section and an insurance section.

The Portuguese Actuaries Institute is a private organization of actuaries which publishes a bulletin with technical articles on timely subjects.

Portuguese branch of the International Association of Insurance Law is a private association and member of the international AIDA. Members are outstanding underwriters, professors, and lawyers who study and promote insurance law.

IX. CHARACTERISTICS OF THE SIXTIES

New Workmen's Compensation Law. A new workmen's compensation law, published in August, 1965, became effective on 19 November 1971 with the regulating decree 360/71. Under the new law all workmen and their families have the right to indemnity for damages from occupational accidents or illnesses. The new rules state that coverage of these risks are transferred from the employers' associations to the underwriters' association except for organizations that have the capacity and solvency to cover the risks themselves.

Export Credit Insurance. In April 1969 the Credit Insurance Company was organized to develop credit insurance on national exports and foreign and domestic credit insurances. It has been recommended that the Company also cover political and commercial risks. Thus it supplements the state guarantee under terms provided by the law.

Study and Elaboration of New Insurance Law. During the last ten years the new insurance law of 12 April 1971 was reviewed. This law has not yet been enforced. It establishes a new system of insurance and reinsurance and creates the National Insurance Board, a consultive branch of the Ministries of Finance and Foreign Affairs regarding enforcing insurance policy in Portugal.

Motor Third Party Liability Required Insurance. This insurance, which has been under study since 1962, is expected to be effected in Portugal shortly. The plan is to initiate a third-party insurance similar to that in other European countries.

Enterprise Reorganization. During recent years insurance companies have updated their operations through modern administration techniques, data processing, and statistics.

X. FUNDAMENTAL LEGISLATION

Chronological Order

21 October 1907—Decree on activities and supervision of insurance industry.

5 November 1929—Decree complementing the above.

5 November 1929—Decree creating the Insurance Inspection Board.

13 December 1932—Decree regulating the Insurance Inspection Board.

31 March 1936—Decree-law on organization and function of Underwriters Association.

23 September 1957—Decree regulating the Credit and Insurance Corporation.

30 June 1961—Decree-law on reserves.

3 April 1969—Decree-law modifying credit insurance system.

12 April 1971—Law regulating insurance activity; creating the National Insurance Board.

By Subjects

General dispositions—decree on activities and supervision of insurance industry, 21 October 1907; decree complementing the above, 5 November 1929; decree-law on reserves, 30 April 1961; law regulating insurance activity, 12 April 1971.

Credit insurance—decree-law modifying credit insurance system, 3 April 1969.

Insurance Inspection Board—decree creating it, 5 November 1929; regulating decree, 13 December 1932.

National Insurance Board—law creating it, 12 April 1971.

Credit and Insurance Corporation—regulating decree, 23 September 1957.

Underwriters Association—decree-law on its organization and functioning, 31 March 1936.

Spain

I. GENERAL INFORMATION

Historical Note. The first ancestors of life insurance in Spain are the disability and old age pensions of the eighteenth century. At the beginning of the nineteenth century a number of urban fire insurance mutuals were created, some of which survive today as important companies. This movement was occurring in other continental nations during this period. A few years later English and French companies began operations in Spain, which initiated the current entrepreneural lines of insurance activities.

In 1864 the oldest and most important of the current insurance companies, La Unión y el Fénix Español, was founded. At the beginning of the twentieth century many insurance companies were organized along with work accident mutuals. This increase in insurance activity caused the publishing of the 1908 insurance law and its 1912 regulation, thus marking the beginning of modern insurance.

Later permanent companies were organized, especially in 1932 and 1933 when the coverage of agricultural occupational risks became mandatory.

Official Control. Control is through the General Subdirection of Insurance, a body created in 1908 and currently a part of the Treasury Ministry. Since its organization it has been called by several names and has been associated with different ministries.

Professional Statute. The most significant example is the National Insurance Union, a public corporation. All insurance entities—stock companies and mutuals—are represented as well as entrepreneurs and employees through their respective national unions and production inspectors and agents through the National Association of Agents. Outstanding for their cohesive work in the market, unions constitute an important institution representing Spanish entrepreneurs and labor.

Market Structure. The market is composed of 670 companies, including a large percentage of medical-surgical, and burial loan companies, and local fire mutuals of limited importance.

When compared with other countries, the insurance market is made up of some two hundred entities whose actual number is decreased by the formation of groups, giving misleading impressions statistically. The index of company concentration is reduced as the first three groups make up approximately 13% of the whole market.

The majority of the companies have their headquarters in Madrid, Barcelona, or Bilbao, with branches in provisional capitals. Normally these companies work through regional or provincial agencies or delegations although there is a tendency to open branches or direct offices.

National companies comprise 76% of the total market; mutuals make up 11% and foreign companies 13%. Automobile insurance represents approximately 40% of the total market, and life insurance is 11%. The remaining 49% is distributed among the remaining branches of private insurance.

International Expansion. With the exception of La Unión y el Fénix, which conducts more than 50% of its operations abroad, international expansion of Spanish insurance has been slow and has even declined in the past fifteen years. However, now a new interest is developing for operating abroad, almost paralleling the increase of foreign trade in Spain.

Workmen's Compensation. In 1966, with the new Social Security plan, occupational accidents and illnesses were separated from private insurance and were provided by labor mutuals and employers' mutuals. The latter were organized following the legal transformation of private insurance mutuals which had to adapt to new conditions. All workmen's compensation is under the Ministry of Labor and is excluded from this study.

Agents and Brokers. Until recently regulation of agents and brokers was unsatisfactory since adequate protection was not provided by arbitration in insurance. The law of private insurance production (30 December 1969) and its regulation (8 July 1971) should alleviate this problem. The contracting system through brokers has not developed except in Barcelona. However North American brokerage firms are being introduced.

Public Insurancce. This is limited to coverage of catastrophic risks (Compensation Consortium) and travellers in collective transport (Comissariat). The coverage of export credit risks (Spanish Consortium and Company of Export Credit Insurance) and traffic risks regarding official vehicles (National Guarantee Fund) is outstanding.

Reinsurance. Autonomous professional reinsurance is not well developed except for large international insurers. Lately, however, the Goya Company has experienced important international growth, especialy in Latin America.

II. FORM AND OPERATION OF PRIVATE INSURERS

Basic Legal Rules. These include the Stock Company Law of 17 July 1951, the Commerce Code of 28 August 1885, the law regulating private insurances of 16 December 1954 and its regulation of 2 February 1912, and the decree on technical reserve investments of 12 September 1970.

Legal Nature. Only stock companies or mutuals are legally authorized.

Social Purpose. This must be limited to insurance and reinsurance operations.

Operations Area. A company may deal in all branches and modalities of insurance simultaneously providing minimum capital and guarantee deposits are fulfilled.

Constitution Requirements. The minimum stock required for national companies is 25,000,000 pesetas ($385,000) disbursed at 50%. Reduced capitals are disbursed for companies working only in secondary branches— 3,000,000 pesetas for illness and burials, health assistance, glass, hailstorms, robbery, or livestock life. Foreign companies have to prove possession in their own country of capital equivalent to that required for Spaniards.

The warrant deposit for both national and foreign companies is 5,000,000 ($76,000) in public state values. Reduced deposits are predicted (600,000 pesetas) for companies operating in only one of the two groups indicated when discussing capital.

In addition, foreign companies must prove that they have 2,000,000 ($30,000) in Spain for overhead.

Process of Authorization. Documentation for both national and foreign companies includes a constitutional writ for stock companies or a founding certificate for mutuals, laws and regulations, technical bases, tariffs and policies. In addition foreign companies must submit a statement of submission to Spanish laws, proof that they are accredited in the country of their origin, balance and profits and loss accounts for the past five years, and designation of the person who will act as principal representative in Spain.

The procedure followed by both national and foreign companies is that they submit themselves to the General Subdirection of Insurance, which is under the Treasury Ministry. When authorization is given, it provides for inscription in the Special Register of Insurance Companies of the General Subdirection. Concession must be granted if legal requirements are met, and against a rejected decision a contentious-administrative appeal may be filed. Authorization is published in the Official State Bulletin. Although authorization may be denied foreign companies when circumstances of the case so advise, in practice there are no rejections.

Reporting Obligations. Both national and foreign companies must submit reports, balance and profits and loss accounts, with complementary states to the General Subdirection of Insurance within six months after the end of the fiscal year. This is followed by publication in the Official Insurance Bulletin of the balances, profits, and loss accounts and relative dispositions of the company. Accounting models are normalized by the General Subdirection of Insurance. Spanish and foreign operations are separated.

III. CONTRACTING

Basic Legal Rules. These include the Regulating Law of Private Insurance of 16 December 1954 and the regulation of 2 February 1912, the Commerce

Code of 28 August 1885, and ministerial orders—16 December 1943 (collective insurance), 13 January 1955 (premium payment), and 3 June 1968 (individual life and accident).

Policies. All policies must be authorized by the General Subdirection of Insurance. The company must present policies, models of proposed insurance, general conditions, particular conditions, and special clauses. Although each company usually drafts its own policies, models of uniform contracts previously drafted by the National Insurance Union are frequently submitted for approval.

Tariffs. All tariffs must be authorized by the General Subdirection of Insurance, which reviews corresponding notes and technical bases for calculation subscribed by an actuary. Theoretically there is freedom in application except in branches subject to specified official regulation where tariffs are the same for all companies. In practice, however, those developed by the National Insurance Union of a uniform nature are usually supervised.

In compulsory automobile insurance tariffs are the same for all companies although deviations up to 18% are authorized; those drafted by the National Insurance Union are also uniform regarding voluntary automobile insurance, transports (hulls), fire, robbery, and glass, among other branches. Merchandise transports, General Civil Responsibility, and Individual Accident insurance are practically free. In life insurance variations depend on where the tables "A.F." or "P.M." are applied since these are used by almost all companies. There is in practice uniformity in types of surcharges for costs of compensation.

Compulsory Insurance. There are three types of insurance which are compulsory because of the type of risk:

1. Required automobile insurance began in 1965 for all motor vehicles. It is based on a plan of objective civil responsibility enabling the victims or claimants to receive direct action against the insuring company. This insurance provides a maximum coverage of 300,000 pesetas per person ($4,600); however, for a disaster, the guarantee is unlimited. The monies above the maximum figure plus the amount of material damages is charged to the Supplementary Civil Responsibility Insurance, integrated into the Voluntary Automobile Branch, in which guilt exists.

2. Compulsory hunting insurance was enforced first in April 1971. It is similar to the compulsory automobile insurance in that it is based on a plan of objective civil responsibility and establishes a direct claim of the victim or claimant against the insurance company to a maximum of 300,000 pesetas per person. The guarantee for disasters, however, is unlimited. The monies above this figure plus the amount for material damages may be covered by ordinary voluntary civil responsibility insurance.

3. Compulsory travelers insurance furnishes indemnification in case of accidents leading to death (up to 400,000 pesetas or $6,100) or disability (up

to 600,000 pesetas) of persons transported by railroad, plane, or automobile if these types of transportation render regular interurban public service. The premium of this insurance is included in the price of the tickets.

Other types of compulsory insurance, includes the following:

1. Catastrophic risks are those produced from extraordinary events such as war, mutiny, revolution, hurricanes, earthquakes, floods, etc. The Insurance Compensation Consortium covers these risks through the insurance companies themselves, and the policies must have a clause to this effect. These companies, when acting as intermediaries between the Consortium and the insurees, provide an additional premium in their policies (20% for hail, 15% for fire, 5% for transport, 3% for robbery, and 1% for individual accident and voluntary automobile insurance). This must be paid to the company periodically.

2. Nuclear risks are those originating from accidents in nuclear installations or from development of activities using ratioactive materials or apparatus causing possible ionizing radiation. The maximum responsibility is 350,000,000 pesetas ($5,400,000). Coverage is provided by the Insurance Compensation Consortium when guarantees covered by private companies fail to reach the minimum civil responsibility provided in the Nuclear Power Law.

3. Risks occurring to travelers using public transportation are covered by the Commissariat of Compulsory Travelers Insurance.

4. Traffic risks occurring to official vehicles are covered through the National Guarantee Fund.

5. Export credit risks are covered by the Spanish Company of Export Credit Insurance, S.A., which has the exclusive concession of covering commercial risks derived from foreign trade and state negotiations covering political and extraordinary risks.

Foreign Insurance Restrictions. Foreign insurance may not be used to cover ships, planes, and vehicles registered in Spain; furnishings and real estate in Spain except for merchandise under international transport regulations; persons and responsibilities of Spaniards living in Spain. It is also illegal to purchase insurance in foreign currency unless authorized by the Treasury Ministry.

IV. TECHNICAL RESERVES

Basic Legal Rules. These include the law of 16 December 1954 regulating private insurance and the regulation of 2 February 1912, the decree of 12 September 1970 on reserve investments, and the 24 May 1971 ministerial order on reserve investments.

Classes. Mathematical (life) classes must be calculated in accordance with technical notes and mortality tables approved for this purpose by the General Subdirection of Insurance. Simplified global calculation is used. This also holds for premium reserves. The law provides for unitary calculations, policy to policy, or simplified global methods providing they do not assume less than 33% of the issued premiums. This system is the one usually followed. In automobile insurance global calculations which presume 40% of the premiums are authorized.

All reserves must be invested in Spain in the following manner: 30% in public state values; 30% in public state values or fixed income values authorized by the Treasury Ministry, or industrial values which meet specified prerequisites, or by participation in funds and security investment companies; 40% in one of the above or in savings banks, regular banks, loans on values, real estate, mortgages, forests or premiums pending payment.

Outstanding losses must cover the global value of all disasters, expired capitals, and income or profits of insurees who have not paid at the end of each fiscal year. Until now the global calculation system has not been permitted on issues premiums, but a new disposition is being studied which authorizes and regulates this procedure.

Investment is the same as that above. The 40% may be used for mathematical reserves and current risks.

Deviations of loss ratio exist in the automobile branch and are called "stabilization reserve." A percentage of the positive technical reserves of the direct insurance is set aside for this (40% in compulsory insurance and 25% in voluntary insurance) until the quantity reaches 30% of the average commercial premiums for the past three fiscal years. Companies may use free investment here.

Value fluctuation is called "reserve for insurees profits." Here are accumulated amounts corresponding to life insurance modalities with the insuree participating in the profits. Investment procedures are the same as for mathematical reserves.

General Requirements of Goods To Be Used as Reserve Covers. For fixed income values, public state values have no limits; other public values and income securities must be quoted on the Stock Exchange and be declared approximate by the Investments Board of the Treasury Ministry.

Variable income values must be quoted on the Stock Exchange at least one hundred days a year; the minimum annual quoting value must be equal to 1.5% of the corporation capital; the average quotation must be no less than 90% of the nominal value; the capital and reserves of the companies invested in must be more than 500 million pesetas ($7,090,000); the funds participations and Security Investment Company shares must be quoted on the Stock Exchange, but they are exempt from other requisites.

Real estate must be finished buildings. However, they may be floors or buildings under construction if the insurer contracts for beginning construction within two years and finishes it within the next three.

General Limits of Investment. Investment in securities through the same entity cannot be more than 10% of the technical reserves (although it can reach 20% when dealing with fund participations or shares belonging to an unregistered investment company) nor more than 10% of values placed in circulation by the entity (unless dealing with a security investment fund. In this event it may reach 20%. When buying shares in a security investment company, it may reach 67%.)

Premiums pending payment are admitted for the amount of technical reserves on the premiums with a 15% limit on those in life insurance. Investment in forests has a 5% limit on the reserves.

V. REINSURANCE

Basic Legal Rules. These include the regulating law of private insurance of 16 December 1954, the decree of 19 September 1944, the 30 December 1944 ministerial order regulating reinsurance operations on Spanish risks, the 24 February 1965 ministerial order on foreign companies; the decrees of 5 July 1945 and 21 March 1952 regulating the official reinsurance committee.

Legal Nature. Only stock companies can provide reinsurance. Mutuals cannot accept reinsurance.

Process of Authorization. Authorization is automatic for national or foreign companies which have been cleared to operate in direct insurance in a particular branch. National companies who provide reinsurance only have to have a minimum capital of 25,000,000 pesetas (about $385,000), disbursed at 50%. Foreign companies which apply for authorization to operate in reinsurance only must present balances and accounts for the past three years (compared to five when proposing to work in direct insurance as well). They must also have an accreditative functioning certificate in their own country, and must provide their social statutes and a list of counsellors and directors. Authorization is obtained easily with no discrimination.

Reporting Obligations. Both national and foreign companies must report to the Spanish Institute of Foreign Currency their annual balances resulting from operations with foreign companies, separated according to direct insurance (accepted and ceded) and reinsurance (accepted and retroceded). Each year foreign companies must send a copy of the General Report-Balance for the fiscal year to the General Insurance Subdirection and a report on reinsurance premiums accepted and retroceded in Spain.

Balances and Remittances in Foreign Currency. A report of balances of reinsurance accounts (cessions or retrocessions) abroad and acceptations from abroad must be made quarterly to the Official Reinsurance Committee. The use of foreign currency in these operations must be authorized by the Spanish Institute of Foreign Currency (IEME).

Official Control. Control comes through the Official Reinsurance Committee of the General Insurance Subdirection, a dependant organ of the

Spanish Institute of Foreign Currency (IEME). The General Insurance Sub-direction may halt or rescind contracts for reinsurance under the following conditions: when monetary speculative operations are revealed, when reciprocity is unavailable, when agreements are made on foreign currency, when it is unavailable or inconvenient to use, and when foreign policy reasons exist.

VI. TAXES

Basic Legal Rules.   These include an adaptation of the rule on general tax on company income and that of other legally recognized groups of 23 December 1967, the General Tax on Company Business of 29 December 1966, The Capital Income Tax of 23 December 1967, article 104 of the 11 June 1964 Law of Tributary Reform, the 8 June 1965 resolution on Direct Taxes General Direction, article 45 of the 16 December 1954 law on Regulation of Private Insurance, the 13 April 1956 regulation on Insurance Compensation Consortium, the 3 October 1964 law-decree creating the National Guarantee Fund, and the 13 May 1965 Ministerial Order on Obligatory Motor Vehicles Insurance.

Taxes and Loadings over Premiums.   A General Tax on Company Business is charged on sales and services applied to the total charged the insuree (premium plus surcharges). It includes a 2% charge on insurance and goods and 1% on insurance on persons. The amount is charged to the insuree.

The Control Organism Rate is a parafiscal tax to defray the expenses of the General Insurance Subdirection. It charges 2% of the net premium in all branches of direct insurance and 0.5% to 1% in reinsurance, and is charged to the insuree.

Nonfiscal surcharges for the Insurance Compensation Consortium varies according to the branch—from 20% of the premium for hail damage to 1% for individual accidents. Surcharges for the National Guarantee Fund of Traffic Risks affect only compulsory automobile insurance and are provisionally fixed at 3%. (see section VIII).

Taxes and Loadings over Profits.   The tax on company income affects both companies and their legal representatives. The encumbrance rate for stock companies is 30% of the profits received each fiscal year. From this quota "taxes on account" are deducted throughout the fiscal year. Mutual companies are in a special category and pay 1.30% on collected premiums in life, accident, marine, and transport insurance and 4.10% on fire and other branches where the purpose is to repair damage to goods or properties. On this quota a variable municipal surcharge is levied, the maximum surcharge being 42%.

A special encumbrance tax is applied to stock companies. This tax, which is similar to the Company Income Tax has a rate of 4% of the profits.

A Capital Income Tax is levied on dividends or interest, including profits paid by insurance companies to their shareholders. The rate is 15% of the dividend value.

VII. PRODUCTION (AGENTS)

Basic Legal Rules. These include the regulating law on private insurance production of 30 December 1969 and the ministerial order regulating the production of private insurance of 8 July 1971.

Kinds of Agents. Free agents act as brokers or professional mediators with no exclusive connection with any particular company. Captive agents are under contract to one company; they may be affiliated with several companies providing they deal in various branches, one branch exclusively for each company.

Representatives are captive agents with specified representational powers granted by the company. Subagents work with and are responsible to agents.

Previous Requirements. All agents must be Spanish citizens legally and morally capable of serving the profession. However, foreigners may act under conditions equal to those required in their countries for Spaniards.

Free agents and representatives must pass certain aptitude tests unless they have the title of actuary or another title assuming knowledge of insurance.

Authorization. Free agents and representatives may obtain the title of agent granted by the Treasury Ministry. Captive agents may acquire the title of agent by signing the agency contract with a company; there is no need of a title. Subagents are named directly by the agents without intervention of the insuring entity.

Bail. Only free agents have to pay bail of 100,000 pesetas ($1,500) fixed by the Insurance Production Regulation of 8 July 1971.

Agency Contracts. These are of a mercantile nature and must contain statements regarding duration and prior notice time for rescinding; demarcation of zones, branches, and faculties and whether or not they are exclusive; remuneration; cession and transmission of portfolio and causes of contract voiding.

Commissions. The commission is fixed by each company except in automobile insurance where a maximum percentage exists for external negotiation costs. Usual commission for provisional agents is 15% on compulsory automobile insurance, 20% on volunteer automobile insurance; 27.5% for fire, robbery and similar branches; 80% on life during the first year with decreasing percentages in successive years, finally reaching 5% in the third or fourth year.

Local agents usually receive 5% to 7% less than the above in diverse branches and 20% less in life during the first year. Conditions frequently are established for subsidies, growth rappels, (obligations to pay an additional contribution) etc., especially for provincial agents. Agents with employees have a right to 55% from Register Rights (surcharges of policy administration) of their portfolio; however, these surcharges are disappearing.

Official Protection. All agents must be associated with the National Agents School and provincial schools integrated in the Insurance Union.

It is illegal to hold a public or private post where authorization, jurisdiction, and faculties represent limitations to the insured regarding contracting and free selection of the insurance company. To date these practices have not occurred and nominations are conducted by companies without requiring professionality; this is being changed with the enactment of the 8 July 1971 regulation.

Portfolio rights include the fact that in a cession the agent will continue receiving part of the commission on premiums. Percentages established in the regulation are 70% for fire and robbery, 40% for illness, and 55% in the remaining branches. Captive agents must work with a company at least three years to acquire this right. In the event of the death of an agent, portfolio rights are transmissible to his heirs as *inter vivos*. In this event the insurance company has a buying option over third parties. If the company merges or cedes its portfolio, agents retain their rights with the new company.

A social security savings bank under the National Agents School is maintained from quotas from associated insurance companies and funds voluntarily contributed by the affiliates themselves. It provides retirement, old age, disability, and orphans' pensions as well as subsidies for accidents and long illnesses.

VIII. INSTITUTIONAL BODIES

Governmental Entities. There are nine of these groups.

The general insurance subdirection is under the Treasury Ministry and it is responsible for supervision of legislative fulfillment of private insurance. It is controlled through the technical corps of inspectors of insurance and savings.

The Insurance Consulting Board is an organ of the General Insurance Subdirection which is responsible for decisions on legislative interpretation, recording of companies, inspection orders, and reseouces to be applied to insurance legislation and legal modification proposals.

The Insurance Arbitration Court is a legal organ comprised of two Supreme Court Magistrates (one of whom acts as president) and a general insurance subdirection technician, who resolve questions arising from interpretation of coverage formulae directly protected by the state, such as compulsory travelers' insurance and catastrophic risks. The Court also has an informative mission regarding litigation cases between insurers and the insured. There is no prejudice or legal rights reserved for civil jurisdiction.

The Spanish Institute of Foreign Currency (IEME) is under the Treasury Ministry and the Bank of Spain. It is responsible for supervising coverage in foreign currency and reinsurance operations abroad through the Official Reinsurance Committee.

The Insurance Compensation Consortium under the General Insurance Subdirection covers catastrophic or extraordinary natural risks affecting goods insured by private company policies. Nuclear risks are covered when guarantees granted by private companies do not reach the legally-established minimum. It also covers some export credit and compulsory reinsurance in the hailstorm branch. (See Contracting: Compulsory Insurance.)

Compulsory Travelers Insurance Commissariat is the organ under the General Insurance Subdirection responsible for transaction and administration of Compulsory Travelers Insurance. (See Contracting: Compulsory Insurance.)

National Fund for Traffic Risks Guarantee is under the General Insurance Subdirection which, related to the compulsory automobile insurance, covers state civil responsibility on official vehicles of the government. It also provides compensation for bodily injury to traffic accident victims when the perpetrator of the accident is unknown or lacks the compulsory insurance certificate without damage to responsible third parties. (See Contracting: Compulsory Insurance.)

The Insurance Mutual of the National Institute of Industry (MUSINI) is a legally private company created in 1968 for coverage of risks; it promotes the prevention and industrial protection of companies in which the said official body participates. MUSINI has a legally limited field of action in these companies. Part of the insured funds are placed in the remaining insurance companies on the market through coinsurance. The maximum placed in each one is in accordance with their limits of acceptance of insurance in national or foreign reinsurance markets.

Spanish Company for Export Credit Insurance, S.A. is a semi-state-owned stock company created by a law of 4 July 1970 and organized on 17 May 1971. It is responsible for direct coverage on commercial risks of foreign trade and political and extraordinary risks for the State derived from trade. Prior to this law political and extraordinary risks were covered by the Insurance Compensation Consortium, and commercial risks were covered by the Cia. Española de Crédito y Caución, S.A., with the State participating in its capital. (See Contracting, Compulsory Insurance.)

Associations. These include the following:

The National Insurance Union is a public body in the union organization. Entrepreneurs are represented in the economic section, workers in the social section, and agents through their national school. Its major function is the preparation of uniform policy tariffs and clauses and the coordination of the market and its institutional improvement. It also helps the union organization in the drafting of proposals on regulation material for work, compensation, etc.

The Union Service for Special Automobile Risks is a group in the National Insurance Union formed voluntarily by insurance companies. Its object is the coverage of compulsory automobile insurance for member companies regarding risks directly ceded to it by these companies because of their special risks. This group also provides "frontier insurance" (automobile).

The Professional Insurance School is a teaching institution provided by the National Insurance Union to train professional insurers. It has branches in Madrid and Barcelona.

The Spanish Tourist Insurance Group is a national range union institution under the Insurance Union responsible for negotiation and administration of tourist insurance. This private and freely contracted insurance covers damages to tourists in Spain themselves or their property, including accidents, illness, legal defense, repatriation of vehicles and occupants, loss of luggage, and civil responsibility from the use of automobiles.

Spanish Automobile Insurers Office (OFESAUTO) is the body in the National Insurance Union responsible for dealing with traffic accidents affecting insurees of companies forming part of the Interbureau Agreement occurring in other countries adhering to the agreement.

Aviation Risks Insurers Group is a private institution representing many insurance companies selling aviation insurance. It attempts to provide maximum collaboration and coordination among the companies, especially in the distribution of coinsurance type risks.

Spanish Section of the International Association of Insurance Law (SEAIDA) is a private association and member of the international AIDA representing insurers, professors, and lawyers. It studies and promotes insurance rights. Several regional groups of this association have been organized.

Center of Iberoamerican Insurance Studies and Research (CIESI) is a private association, which has as its goal, the organization of seminars and meetings, as well as the study and promotion of research, regarding Iberoamerican Insurance. It is a member, with all rights, of the Hemispheric Conference for Insurance.

Cooperative Research among Insuring Entities (ICEA) is a private association of most insurance companies which provides publications, courses, and seminars on the managerial, commercial, and administrative aspects of insurance.

The Spanish Actuaries Institute is a private association of actuaries which has published several technical publications in its field.

Other organizations include the Spanish Association of Claims Liquidators, the Accident Prevention Association, and the Spanish Maritime Commissariat.

IX. CHARACTERISTICS OF THE SIXTIES

Implementation of Compulsory Automobile Insurance. Compulsory automobile civil responsibility insurance, created by the law of 24 December 1962, went into effect in May 1965. This insurance, planned to cover material and personal damages from vehicle traffic, has been applied only for bodily injury. Action has been established based on the risk theory of objective responsibility and not on the extracontractual guilt system. This also provided for a national bail fund for coverage of official vehicles and for compensation when no insurance exists or the person causing damage is unknown.

Another first for this insurance has been the unification of the special Conditions "certified", and identical insuring conditions for the whole market. The fact that compensation for legal authority is higher than the limits of this insurance and therefore come under the Voluntary Automobile Civil Responsibility Insurance, has caused technical and administrative difficulties for insurance companies.

Automobile Insurance Expansion. Automobile insurance has become the most important insurance on the market becuase of the automotive industry, the increased number of automobiles on the road, and the implementation of compulsory automobile insurance.

Work Accidents Insurance Socialization. In 1966 a new rule of Social Security was enforced which segregated work accidents from private insurance and placed them under labor mutuals and employer mutuals. This created a loss of $77 million for private insurance companies and caused reconstruction which markedly affected some insurance companies.

Investment Liberalization. The decree of 12 September 1970 marked an outstanding landmark comparable to the 1908 Insurance Law, which helped Spain take its place among other nations in this field. Life insurance, which up to this time had been underdeveloped, received new opportunities.

Basic changes include (1) increased opportunities for investment, including variable income quoted on the Stock Exchange for coverage of 70% of mathematical reserves and current risks, and 100% of pending disasters. Coverage of these value reserves had been limited to fixed income securities or public funds; (2) encouragement for real estate investment; (3) admission of construction sites; (4) admission of premiums pending on reserves.

Decartelization of the Market. The General Insurance Subdirection has authorized tariffs individually proposed by companies which has initiated an elimination process for uniform compulsory tariff systems. This has introduced the factor of price competition in Spanish insurance and a greater concern for the needs of clients and changes determined by modern business.

Creation of the INI Insurance Mutual (MUSINI). In 1968 the National

Industry Institute and its companies created MUSINI which is legally a mutual but really a selfinsurance cooperative for companies of this body. These are usually the largest Spanish companies in the industrial field. Since this implies possible future extention of private insurance activities, these insurers are obligated to improve industrial coverage to the maximum. Policies subscribed by MUSINI are ceded in coinsurance to the companies which operate in the market; thus, more companies participate in large industrial risks.

Reduction of Sales Tension. The rising insurance demand, particularly automobile insurance, enables insurers to increase their business without individual sales efforts. The greater costs of inspection personnel have effected an important reduction of sales pressure on the public. This brings about a better administration and cost reduction.

Deprofessionalization of Agents. In the '60s a crisis in the insurance profession was produced. Many professional salesmen left the field, and many who continued drew the major part of their income from other work. The primary cause for this was the loss of occupational insurance, which had been a major source of income for agents, and the introduction of new distribution methods in automobile insurance through concessionaires and finance companies. This was caused by lack of effective regulation in the profession and the potential for agents in other intermediary activities.

New Personnel Policy. Class-conscious workers have been demanding their rights, especially from such service organizations as banks where they have received salary improvements. This causes insurers to be more concerned over work productivity. Similarly a change has been produced by the younger generation of directive personnel, who are more prepared to resolve problems of a competitive market, growing cost of personnel, necessity of reform, and to plan for the future.

Entrepreneural Reorganization. , Insurance companies have tended to decentralize functions and services and introduce computerization, and generally have become better organized in the last decade.

X. FUNDAMENTAL LEGISLATION

Chronological Order

1 February 1912—Royal decree approving regulation on register and inspection of insurance companies.

29 September 1944—decree regulating mercantile reinsurance operations.

5 July 1945—decree regulating official reinsurance committee.

10 August 1953—ministerial order approving regulation of insurance Arbitration Court.

16 December 1954—Law regulating private insurance.

13 April 1956—decree approving regulation of Insurance Compensation Consortium.

24 December 1962—law of use and circulation of motor vehicles (automobile insurance).

22 October 1964—decree regulating tourist insurance.

19 November 1964—decree approving compulsory automobile insurance regulation.

10 September 1966—decree regulating export credit insurance.

22 July 1967—decree regulating nuclear risk insurance.

11 October 1967—decree approving the regulation of the National Guarantee Fund (automobile insurance).

21 March 1968—decree approving text based on compulsory automobile insurance.

6 March 1969—decree approving regulation of compulsory travelers insurance Commissariat.

30 December 1969—law regulating private insurance production.

4 July 1970—law modifying the regime of export credit insurance.

12 September 1970—decree on technical reserve investment.

4 April 1971—decree regulating compulsory hunting insurance.

24 May 1971—ministerial order on reserves investment.

8 July 1971—ministerial order regulating private insurance production.

By Subject

General dispositions—law regulating private insurance, 16 December 1954; royal decree approving regulation on registration and inspection of insurance companies, 2 February 1912; law regulating private insurance production, 30 December 1969; decree on technical reserves investment, 12 September 1970; ministerial order on reserves investment, 24 May 1971; ministerial order regulating private insurance production, 8 July 1971.

Export Credit Insurance—regulating decree, 10 September 1966; law modifying regime of credit export insurance, 4 July 1970; law on use and circulation of motor vehicles, 24 December 1962; decree approving text founded on law, 21 March 1968; decree approving regulation of compulsory insurance, 19 November 1964; decree approving regulation of National Guarantee Fund, 11 October 1967.

Tourist insurance—regulating decree, 22 October 1964.

Nuclear risk insurance—regulating decree, 22 July 1967.

Reinsurance—regulating decree of mercantile insurance operations, 29 September 1944; regulating decree of official reinsurance committee, 5 July 1945.

Insurance Arbitration Court—ministerial order approving the regulation, 10 August 1953.

Compulsory hunting insurance—regulating decree, 4 April 1971.

Insurance Compensation Consortium—decree approving regulation, 13 April 1956.

Compulsory Travelers Insurance Commissariat—decree approving regulation, 6 March 1969.

Uruguay

I. GENERAL INFORMATION

Historical Note. The development of insurance in Uruguay was begun during the second half of the twentieth century. However, mutual societies go back as far as 1852, and the first Uruguayan company was organized in 1854. Legislation in 1859 and 1860 covers activities of underwriters, requiring insurance companies to pay a license and stamp tax. The Commercial Code was passed in 1866.

Until 1910 foreign companies were important, selling three times as many premiums as national companies. This led to the law of 27 December 1911 creating a state body, the Insurance Bank of Uruguay, which controlled most insurance activity.

Official Control. The only "control" is the outstanding role of the Insurance Bank of Uruguay.

Professional Statute. The Fire Underwriters Committee is the only body concerned. This association of all fire insurance companies seeks the defense of common interests of associates.

Market Structure. Private companies may operate only in lines not monopolized by the government. The market is comprised of one national and sixteen foreign companies in addition to the State Insurance Bank. More than 80% of the insurance written in Uruguay is by the State Insurance Bank.

International Expansion. This is practically nonexistent.

Workmen's Compensation. This insurance is monopolized by the State Insurance Bank and the law of 23 November 1961 makes it compulsory. By law 13.705 of 22 November 1958 a pension on rural producers for subordinate workmen was transferred from the State Insurance Bank to the Social Security Bank.

Agents and Brokers. They have no relevant significance from the point of view of private insurance due to characteristics of the market in Uruguay. The State Insurance Bank has agents throughout Uruguay. Brokers other than agents who contribute business to the Bank are not Bank employees.

Public Insurance. This is provided by the State Insurance Bank.

Reinsurance. This has not been professionally developed. Except for one private national company and the State Insurance Bank, no other company operates in reinsurance in a strict sense.

II. FORM AND OPERATION OF PRIVATE INSURERS

Basic Legal Rules. These include the law of 27 December 1911 creating the State Insurance Bank, the decree of 18 April 1914 enforcing the monopoly on workmen's compensation insurance, the law of 19 December 1926 enforcing various monopolies, the law of 7 December 1961 on operation of insurance companies.

Legal Nature. This is through stock companies.

Social Purpose. This is limited to insurance operations.

Operations Area. This is limited to lines not monopolized by the State Insurance Bank. Private companies must comply with requirements of guarantee deposits.

Constitution Requirements. No minimum stock requirements are specified. Both foreign and national companies, however, shall make a warrant deposit in the Bank of the Republic to the joint order of the Executive Power, the following amounts in public debt or mortgage titled of Uruguay valued at the rate quoted in the Stock Exchange the day prior to deposit: (1) 10,000 pesos for companies dealing in agriculture insurance and breakage of windows. If they operate on both risks, disposition of item (3) shall apply. (2) 20,000 pesos for companies in other classes of insurance if they deal in only one type of risk. (3) 30,000 pesos for companies writing fire insurance policies. Companies operating in more than one risk must deposit an additional 5,000 pesos for each of the risks underwritten. The principal risk is considered that with the highest guarantee indicated and for which the full guarantee is deposited. Companies ceasing operations will recover their deposits.

Any foreign company must invest a minimum of 150,000 pesos in addition to the warrant deposit without counting the above-mentioned items. It will be equalized to national companies regarding tax payments on income and on referred deposit. Investments may be in real estate or public debt or mortgage titles issued by the Mortgage Bank of Uruguay valued at the rate quoted by the Stock Exchange the day prior to the deposit.

Process of Authorization. No specified norms refer to documentation. The Executive Power grants authorization. An announcement is published in the Official Gazette for fifteen days. Claims may be made before the State Insurance Bank within the thirty-one days from the date of first publication.

Reporting Obligations. A statement of operations of the preceding month must be sent to the Reception Office of License Tax during the first eight days of each month. Also, a list of persons authorized to contract insurance and receive premiums and the agency address must be sent the same office every six months.

III. CONTRACTING

Basic Legal Rules. These include the Commerce Code of 25 June 1861, the organic law of State Insurance Bank of 27 December 1911, the State Insurance Bank regulation of 31 January 1912, the law of 28 February 1941 on workmen's compensation and occupational diseases, aeronautic legislation code, the law of 25 June 1946 on fire insurance and elevator damages, the law of 23 November 1961 declaring workmen's compensation insurance to be mandatory.

Policies. Policies are usually created by the State Insurance Bank.

Rates. These, too, are established by the State Insurance Bank. Law 13.893 of 19 October 1970 on the construction industry, establishes a system regarding uniformity of employers' and workers' contributions to cover various concepts, including workmen's compensation insurance.

Compulsory Insurances. Three risks must be covered: (1) workmen's compensation and occupational disease insurance—this was declared mandatory by a law of 23 November 1961. It includes all manual workmen, commerce and industry employees, rural workers, and domestic service workers, public officials. The state, government departments and other autonomous corporations are required to insure in the Insurance Bank members of their staffs who do manual work. (2) Aviation insurance—crew, passengers, aircrafts, and aviation material must be covered in commercial aviation. Insurance is also mandatory against third party or property damage, up to 100,000 pesos. (3) Fire insurance and elevator damage—This is required for all buildings subject to horizontal property regulation.

The mandatory insurances listed above must be carried with the State Insurance Bank. Risks such as workmen's compensation and occupational diseases, windows, live stock, third-party liability, hailstone, agricultural, civil disturbance, rent guarantee also must be insured in the Insurance Bank.

Foreign Insurance Restrictions. None exists.

IV. TECHNICAL RESERVES

Basic Legal Rules. No legal disposition sets norms for technical reserve calculations. Since only one Uruguayan company operates abroad (apart from the Insurance Bank), the absence of legislation has caused no inconvenience.

Classes. The Insurance Bank operates in the following manner: Norms for mathematical reserve calculation in life insurance correspond to traditional actuary science. Reserves are calculated for current risks and outstanding losses. They are also calculated in the usual way. Ratio deviations of cost of losses to premiums earned are covered by amounts which are designated annually to a contingency reserve. Fluctuation of values is covered by accounting for such property in the balance sheet conservatively.

Requirements of Goods Used as Reserve Covers. In the absence of legal dispositions, norms are established by the Insurance Bank (Art. 17, paragraph c), and (Art. 18 of Organic Charger of 27 December 1911). Art. 83 of Law 13.728 (National Housing Plan) may be cited as an exception: all institutions performing insurance operations must complete their reserves in adjustable mortgage obligations in the percentages established by the Central Bank of Uruguay.

Limits of Investment. None specified.

V. REINSURANCE

Basic Legal Rules. None specified.

Present Statute. Except for the National Company and Insurance Bank, the companies (foreign agencies) do not reinsure because they send abroad excesses of their local expenses in the form of premiums; reinsurance is regulated by their respective head offices. The National Company and the Insurance Bank place their reinsurance abroad on the traditional international market through faculative contracts. A recent disposition of the Central Bank (2 March 1972) states that only two national insurance companies may buy the necessary exchange at the fluctuating quotation of the financial market for remitting abroad the net balances originated by reinsurance of policies issued in Uruguayan currency. For policies issued in foreign currency (since the government authorizes insurers to obtain premium values through the same financial market) the corresponding reinsurance must be paid out of these funds.

VI. TAXES

Basic Legal Rules. These include the law on business licenses (Art. 12) of 28 December 1933, the income tax law of income of capital societies of 21 December 1967, and the law of 7 December 1961 on taxes on insurance companies.

Taxes and Loadings over Premiums. National companies pay a 5% tax on all gross premiums except marine insurance, which is 2% and life which is 0.5%. Foreign companies pay 7%, 4%, and 2% respectively except when they prove a minimum investment in Uruguay of 150,000 pesos. In this event, they pay the same as national companies. The State Insurance Bank is exempt from license, stamps, and seals and of payment of contributions on real estate of their property occupied by their own offices. Agricultural insurance operations are exempted from this licese. A 10% additional license is paid by companies and insurance agencies including the State Insurance Bank.

Taxes and Loadings over Profits. Legal bodies pay an annual tax of 10% on income of the fiscal year.

VII. PRODUCTION (AGENTS)

Basic Legal Rule. This is the Commerce Code of 25 June 1861.

Kinds of Agents. General agents represent the State Insurance Bank in all acts and contracts necessary to perform in different sections of the country. Hail agents tend to matters of hailstone insurance solely. Some general agents are affiliated with the Branch Department and agencies of the Insurance Bank.

Previous Requirements. An agent must be of legal age. Contracts of civil societies or stock companies are reviewed by the legal department of the Insurance Bank which approves or refuses the amendments.

Authorization. The branch department and agencies appoint representatives and the Bank Board of Directors grants or denies authorization.

Bail. Bail funds come through deposit of public debt and mortgage titles or bail insurances contracted in the State Insurance Bank.

Agency Contracts. The Bank grants a representation mandate to general agents which may be revoked at any time. The agent can resign whenever he considers convenient (Art. 12 of the mandate).

Commissions. A commission which is a percentage on premiums on insurances contracted goes to all bank brokers. In addition a 4% commission is calculated on insurance premiums for processing expenses and collection.

Official Protection. None exists.

VIII. INSTITUTIONAL BODIES

Governmental Bodies. Inspection of finance and stock companies is conducted by the department of the Minister of Finance, who is in charge of assisting public powers, controlling and supervising stock companies, and advising prior to the approval of laws and reforms.

The State Insurance Bank is the state body created in 1911 to exercise monopoly over all risks. Various monopolies were effected by decrees up to 1936; now risks monopoliced by the Bank are workmen's compensation and occupational disease, windows, live stock, third-party liability, hail, agricultural, commotion, and similar risks, and rent guarantee. All other lines (fire, life, marine, operate through private institutions. The Insurance Bank was organized with a capital of 3 million pesos, which was increased to 10 million by law of 23 January 1948. Bank administration is headed by a Board consisting of a chairman and four directors appointed by the president of the republic in accordance with the Board of Ministers prior meeting of the Chamber of Senators. Duties of the board are to comply and fulfill stated functions, to examine and approve monthly and annual balances, and to solve matters submitted by its members. The General Manager who serves as attorney of the Board of Directors, executes board resolutions. Because its production volume is estimated at more than 80% of the total market, in practice it controls all insurance companies in the country.

Associations. The Local Committee of Fire Insurance Underwriters was founded on 11 August 1897 to integrate fire insurance companies operating in Uruguay and to establish a local premium rate to protect common interests. The International Association of Insurance Law is the national branch of AIDA and is composed of outstanding professors, lawyers, actuaries, and underwriters. Its object is the study and promotion of insurance law.

IX. CHARACTERISTICS OF THE SIXTIES

The most important events during 1960–70 are the following: the law of 23 November 1961 establishing mandatory workmen's compensation insurance; new standards on operation of insurance companies, established by law of 7 December 1961; and transfer of workmen's compensation and occupational disease coverage to the Social Security Bank, established by law of 22 November 1968. This risk was formerly covered by the State Insurance Bank.

X. FUNDAMENTAL LEGISLATION

Chronological Order

25 June 1861–Commerce Code of the Republic of Uruguay.

27 July 1911–Organic Law of State Insurance Bank (No. 3.935).

31 January 1912–State Insurance Bank Regulation.

8 April 1914–Decree enforcing the monopoly of workmen's compensation insurance.

19 July 1926–Law declaring various monopolies effective (No. 7.975).

30 August 1926–Decree enforcing the insurance monopoly on windows, livestock, third-party liability, hail, agricultural risks, civil disturbance and similar risks and rent guarantee.

28 December 1933–Business License Law.

20 August 1936–Law eliminating possibility of introducing monopolies by government decrees.

28 February 1941–Workmen's compensation and occupational disease law.

25 June 1946–law of fire insurances and elevator damages.

23 January 1948–Law increasing to 10 million the capital of State Insurance Bank.

23 November 1961—Law making workmen's compensation insurance mandatory.

7 December 1961—Law on insurance companies' income.

7 December 1961—Law on income tax of capital societies.

22 November 1968—Law on pension to rural producers whereby workmen's compensation and occupational disease cover for workers is transferred from the State Insurance Bank to the Social Security Bank (13.705).

By Subjects

General Dispositions—Commerce Code of the Republic of Uruguay, 23 June 1861; law declaring various monopolies effective, 19 July 1926; decree enforcing monopoly on insurances on windows, livestock, third-party liability, hail, agricultural risks, commotion and similar risks, and rent bail, 30 August 1926; law eliminating possibility of introducing monopolies by government decree, 20 August 1936; law on insurance companies operations, 7 December 1961.

State Insurance Bank—Insurance Bank organic law, 27 December 1911; Insurance Bank regulation, 31 January 1912; law increasing to 10 million pesos the State Insurance Bank capital, 23 January 1948.

Taxes—Business license law, 28 December 1933; law on insurance companies' income tax, 7 December 1961; law on income tax of capital societies, 21 December 1967.

Workmen's compensation—decree enforcing monopoly of workmen's compensation insurance, 8 April 1914; law on workmen's compensation and occupational diseases, 28 February 1941; law making workmen's compensation insurance compulsory, 23 November 1961; law on pension to rural producers whereby workmen's compensation and occupational disease covering said workers are transferred from the State Insurance Bank to the Social Security Bank, 22 November 1968; law on fire insurances and elevator damages, 25 June 1946.

Venezuela

I. GENERAL INFORMATION

Historical Note. The first Venezuelan insurance company, formed at Maracaibo in 1866, was Compañia de Seguros Marítimos del Zulia (Marine Insurance Company on Zulia). The Commercial Code of Law of 1919 set up the first norms of organization, and the control of insurance companies' investments. In 1935 the first law was passed regarding supervision of insurance companies. This was to be provided by the Fiscal Authority, which was replaced by the Superintendency of Insurance in 1965. In 1938 and 1948 a new law and its regulation were published for insurance operations, which served until the Law of June 1956 went into force.

Official Control. Control is provided by the Superintendency of Insurance through the Ministry of Production (ministerio de Fomento) which not only supervises but also helps fulfill legal dispositions on underwriters' activities, even functioning as arbitrator when requested by interested parties such as underwriters, agents, and insured parties.

Professional Statute. This is provided by the National Insurance Advisory Board, which is made up of one representative from each insurance and reinsurance company in Venezuela, the Superintendent of Insurance, the Chamber of Underwriters of Venezuela, the Venezuelan College of Insurance Agents and Brokers, and the Venezuelan Chamber of the Insurance Brokers Society.

Market Structure. The market consists of thirty-eight companies, three of which deal exclusively in reinsurance. Seventeen companies have guarantee capital and are exclusively Venezuelan, fifty-one companies have Venezuelan capital, and the rest of the companies had till July 1973 to show that most of their capital is Venezuelan. The leading insurance lines are life and fire, which cover 30% and 21% of the market respectively. Most insurance companies have their home office in Caracas.

International Expansion. Some large private insurance companies have branch offices in the Netherland Antilles.

Workmen's Compensation. This insurance is not mandatory. The Social Security system was organized in 1944 and was assigned to the Venezuelan Institute of Social Security.

Agents and Brokers. Intermediary activities is effected through agents, brokers, or broker societies.

Public Insurance. This is undeveloped to date.

Reinsurance. Reinsurance is controlled by the Superintendent, who supervises acceptances, retentions, and cessions of reinsurance companies. He may legally limit or prohibit acceptance or require reinsurance of certain risks if this is considered to be in the best interest of the market as a whole.

II. FORM AND OPERATION OF PRIVATE INSURERS

Basic Legal Rules. These include the Commerce Code of Law of 19 December 1919, the law of insurance and reinsurance companies of 28 June 1965, and corresponding regulations of 5 March 1969.

Legal Nature. The only authorized representation is through a stock company. Although there are no mutual companies nor cooperatives, their existence is foreseen through special laws regulating their operation.

Social Purpose. It is the performance of insurance and reinsurance operations.

Operations Area. A company may operate in all insurance lines simultaneously provided minimum capital requirements are met. The life and financial guarantee insurance cannot be operated at the same time.

Constitution Requirements. Minimum stock requirements include the following: 3,000,000 bolivars ($660,000) to operate in life insurance or general insurances; 4,000,000 to operate in both groups simultaneously, 5,000,000 for companies operating in financial guarantee insurances, and 8,000,000 for those working simultaneously in general insurances and financial guarantee insurances.

Fifty percent of this capital must be in cash when starting operations. Since July 1973 the Law of Insurances and Reinsurances of 1965 requires that a minimum of 51% of the guarantee capital be the property of Venezuelan individuals or corporations.

Warrant deposits are required as follows: 400,000 bolivars ($90,000) if operating in life or general insurance; 500,000 for financial guarantee insurance, 800,000 for life and general insurances; and 900,000 for general insurances and financial guarantee insurances. A minimum of 25% of these deposits must be in securities issued or guaranteed by the federal government; the balance may be invested in currency, mortgage certificates, or national industrial or commercial securities which are authorized by the Superintendency.

Process of Authorization. Documentation requires knowledge of the laws, constitution and deed of the insurance company. After the Superintendent approves the initial resolution, he must have on file model forms of budgets, policies, contracts, receipts and such technical documents as premium tables, commission rates, expenditure estimates for installation and promotion (which must not be above 20% of the disbursed guarantee capital), amortization process for such expenses (between 10 and 20%), and technical plans of operation and account of shareholders.

Authorization procedure involves the following: After the Superintendent approves the above, authorization to operate must be requested and appropriate documents presented within six months of the date when the initial resolution was published. Within the next thirty days the Minister of Production will issue the final resolution to be published in the official gazette and inscribed in the Register of the Superintendency. If operations are not begun within three months, the authorization expires. However, an appeal can be made to the Ministry of Production. The president of the republic can refuse to certify new insurance companies if the economic situation or market conditions make this seem advisable.

Reporting Obligations.   The annual report including a statement of profits and losses, balance and appendixes of statistical accounts must be presented to the Superintendent within the first ninety days of the fiscal year. The annual report, balance sheets, and accounts are published in the newspapers after approval. Standard accounting forms are available from the Superintendent.

III. CONTRACTING

Basic Legal Rules.   These are the Law of Insurance and Reinsurance Companies of 28 June 1965 and its regulation of 6 March 1969.

Policies.   Policies and amendments must be approved by the Superintendent Of Insurance. Uniform policies exist in some lines such as fire, automobile, hull, and R.C. vehicles.

Rates.   No compulsory rate exists. The Insurance Superintendent approves all rates and their amendments. Flexibility of rates exists only when the risks involved do not permit a uniform rate.

Compulsory Insurances.   The Ministry of Communication has a new law under consideration for overland travel which is probably the forerunner of a compulsory third-party liability for vehicles.

Foreign Insurance Restrictions.   No insurances may be written abroad in the following instances: for vessels, planes, and other vehicles registered in Venezuela; for real estate in Venezuela; for persons closing contracts abroad while living in Venezuela. If due to special circumstances insurance cannot be contracted with authorized companies in Venezuela, the Superintendent may authorize foreign insurance.

IV. TECHNICAL RESERVES

Basic Legal Rules.   This includes the law for insurance and reinsurance companies of 28 June 1965 and its regulation of 6 March 1939.

Class.   Life insurance is calculated according to the formulas of final risk reserves and of the balance, as approved by the Superintendent. Premium reserves calculations vary according to insurance line—for general insurances it is no less than 40% of the net fiscal year premiums; for financial securities, it is no less than 60% of the premiums; for undertakers' insurances, it is no less than 1/52 of the premiums.

Outstanding losses for life insurance is called "Reserves for Outstanding Payments" and is calculated on the total of insured capital, outstanding payments for claims or expirations, liquidated surrenders, expired incomes, and other profits of beneficiaries or contracting parties. Outstanding losses for general insurance is called "Reserves for Settlement of Outstanding Losses" and is calculated on the total of losses pending settlement on 31 December, excluding motor third party liability. Here the reserve must be no less than the average cost of losses multiplied by the number of outstanding losses.

Outstanding losses for financial guarantees are calculated on the total of the sums guaranteed or endorsements expired and not paid by 31 December.

Deviations of loss ratio exists only as "Contingent Reserves" in financial security insurance. It is composed of a minimum of 10% of net annual profit until an equal or greater amount of paid capital is reached.

No special system exists for fluctuation of values.

Premium reserves of security companies must be invested in the following manner: (1) no less than 40% in bank deposits, (2) between 10 and 20% in government obligations, (3) not more than 50% in shares or obligations of stock companies. Technical reserves of life and premium reserves of general insurances must be invested as follows: (1) no less than 20% in real estate, industrial or agricultural mortgage certificates, or shares and obligations of stock companies; (2) no more than 50% in institutions or banks, pawn loans, mortgage security loans of first rank on urban buildings, urban constructed property, (3) no less than 30% in values issued or guaranteed by the nation, region, or municipality.

Requirements of Goods To Be Used as Covers. Investments must be in shares or securities of accredited solvent Venezuelan companies or foreign companies which conduct the major part of their business in Venezuela. In both instances they must be approved by the Superintendent. Furthermore, insurance companies are not permitted to invest in organizations in which they have a decisive interest.

General Limits of Investments. Guaranteed loans against security are limited to 70% of the property value. Mortgage loan security is limited to 60% of buildings. Investment on urban property must not exceed 15% of the total reserves and/or be more than 75% of the value of the property.

V. REINSURANCE

Basic Legal Rules. These include the law of insurance and reinsurance companies of 28 June 1965 and its regulation of 8 March 1969.

Legal Nature. It is limited exclusively to a company.

Process of Authorization. The process is similar to that for companies operating in direct insurance with the following exceptions: (1) the subscribed capital must not be less than 4,000,000 bolivars ($880,000). Fifty percent of this must be in cash. A security deposit of 500,000 bolivars is also required. (2) Documents submitted for the approval of the Superintendent must indicate the system of risk acceptances, procedure for currency conversion, the system of retrocessions and calculation of technical reserves.

Reporting Obligations. Before 15 November each year insurance companies must disclose to the Superintendent the net retension for the forthcoming fiscal year, the accepting company's capacity through mandatory reinsurance contracts, and total volume for premium retentions. The following must be submitted to the Superintendent annually before 31 January: report of accepting companies with whom compulsory reinsurance contracts have been signed plus data on the nature of the reinsurance risks, geographical limits of the contract, amount of retentions, maximum reinsurance liability, economic conditions of the contract, calculation system of reserves, and term of accounts. The company must submit a list of assigners, retroceding companies, retrocessionaires plus the above material to the Superintendent before 31 March. Approved reinsurance transactions must be divided into life, transport, fire, accident, casualty, and surety. Most rules applicable to direct insurance companies apply to reinsurance companies.

Official Control. Control is through the Insurance Superintendent, a division of the Ministry of Production. Its operations are similar to direct insurance except that reinsurance is imposed by the Superintendent whenever the risk may affect the stability of an enterprise, acceptances and retrocessions are limited to lines of the stated direct insurance, and reinsurance acceptances may be limited or prohibited by the Superintendent.

VI. TAXES

Basic Legal Rules. These are the law and regulation on income tax and municipal license.

Taxes and Loadings over Premiums. None apply.

Taxes and Loadings over Profits. No information is available.

VII. PRODUCTION (AGENTS)

Basic Legal Rules. These include the insurance and reinsurance law of 28 June 1965 and the regulation of this law of 6 March 1969.

Kinds of Agents. Agents are persons who act directly and exclusively for an insurance or brokerage company. Brokers are persons who act directly but not exclusively for an insurance company. Brokerage societies are companies that act directly or through agents; they are not restricted to one particular insurance company. Insurance companies also may act as production intermediaries without authorization from the Supervisory Office.

Previous Requirements. Agents must pass an examination of professional competence unless they have satisfactorily completed a course in an institute recognized by the Supervisory Office or have served as executive in an insurance company within the past five years. They must have no penal record. They must be authorized by the insurance or brokerage company for which they work. And they must have commercial competence.

Brokers must have three years' experience as an authorized agent or worked in insurance production with the Supervisory Office, an insurance company, or a brokerage company for two consecutive years. They must be of legal age and pass an examination of professional competency similar to that for agents.

Brokerage societies must be a partnership, stock company or limited company; located in Venezuela and maintaining a public office, producing insurance as its principal purpose; its directors must pass an examination for agents and brokers.

Authorization. Authorization is provided by the Supervisory Office, which lists them in a register of agents, brokers, or brokerage societies. Authorization can be revoked for agents and brokers if their production is less than twelve policies of 12,000 bolivares. It is revoked for brokerage societies if they gain more income from activities other than insurance during any fiscal year.

Bail. Brokers and brokerage societies must maintain a bail bond proportionate to commissions paid in the previous fiscal year. This is established in the bylaw of the Insurance and Reinsurance Law, whose minimum and maximum limits are 12,500 and 450,000 bolivares; bail bond must be no less than 5,000 bolivares for brokers and 10,000 for brokers societies.

Agency Contract. The contents of this commercial contract are not expressly regulated by the Insurance Law or bylaw.

Commissions. Commissions are not set by the Supervisory Office. Companies recognize no general minimums or maximums. Insurance companies submit applicable commissions to the Supervisory Office. These must be "within the limits of a healthy administration." The Supervisory Office may modify the commissions statute approved by a company if it deems it necessary.

Official Protection. Protection is provided by the Venezuelan College of Insurance Agents and Brokers and the Venezuelan Chamber of Insurance Brokerage Societies. Functions of these groups are described in Section VIII.

The following individuals are not permitted to serve as insurance agents or brokers: public functionaries; administrators or employees of banks, credit institutions, etc. (this applies to such companies themselves); inspectors of risks, claim adjusters, and assessors; reinsurance intermediaries.

No special rulings cover portfolio rights.

VIII. INSTITUTIONAL BODIES

Governmental Bodies.   The Insurance Supervisory Office within the Ministry of Development is entrusted with observing private insurance operations. Control is through a body of inspectors. It is also a mediator helping resolve differences between companies or between companies and intermediaries, beneficiaries, etc. when mutually requested.

The National Insurance Board is formed by the Insurance Superintendent and a representative from each insurance and reinsurance company controlled by the law. A president, vice-president, and secretary are elected each year from among its members. Their primary functions are to (1) study the economic condition of the country regarding insurance activities and communicate their findings and recommendations to the national executive through the Supervisory Office, (2) inform on consultations with the executive, (3) study and attempt to coordinate and improve the practice of insurance, (4) list private industrial and commercial securities suitable for covering reserves. The Board must present an annual report of its activities to the Ministry of Development.

Associations.   The Venezualan Chamber of Insurers unites most companies and has the following objectives: (1) development, diffusion, and promotion of private insurance, (2) adjustment of companies, (3) the study of tariffs and stipulation of rates for special risks based on collective experience, commercial practice, and development of the profession in Venezuela.

The Venezuelan College of Insurance Agents and Brokers is a private association which unites most agents and brokers to defend its associates, their professional training, and representation before public bodies and officials. It also promotes agents' and brokers' activities.

The Venezuelan Chamber of Insurance Brokerage Companies is similar to the above college and unites brokerage groups constituted in the form of companies.

IX. CHARACTERISTICS OF THE SIXTIES

New Legal Statute.   The most notable event is the enactment and enforcement of the law and bylaw on insurance and reinsurance of 1965 and 1969 respectively. This law governs technical, administrative, commercial, and financial aspects of Venezuelan insurance companies. The law provides that as of 1973 a minimum of 51% of capital stock of insurance and reinsurance companies must be in companies or persons of Venezuelan nationality. It also provides that if economic or market conditions make it necessary, the president of the republic with the Cabinet of Ministers may prevent the establishment of new insurance companies.

X. FUNDAMENTAL LEGISLATION

This includes the Code of Commerce of 19 December 1919, the Insurance and Reinsurance Company Law of 28 June 1965, and the bylaw of the above of 6 March 1969.

Appendix I

GENERAL CONSIDERATIONS OF THE WHOLE STUDY

The following is a comparative summary of the countries included in this book. The primary aim is to look at the most important aspects discussed so that the reader can have a quick and complete view. Because of the brevity of this appendix, the reader should not form final conclusions without consulting the individual chapters.

Legal Nature of Insurance Companies. The stock company is recognized only in Bolivia, Paraguay, Peru, Uruguay, and Venezuela. The statute of stock company or cooperative enterprise is authorized in Brazil, Colombia, and Ecuador. The stock company and the mutual association is permitted in Spain, Mexico, and Portugal. The systems of stock company, cooperative enterprise, or mutual association are authorized in Argentina and Chile.

Social Purpose. The social purpose of insuring companies in all countries in this study is exclusively that of operations of insurance and/or reinsurance.

Operations Area. Insurance companies may operate simultaneously in all branches if prior conditions are met in Argentina, Bolivia, Brazil, Ecuador, Spain, Mexico, Paraguay, Peru, and Portugal.

Minimum Capital. Minimum capital is required (in different amounts and according to branches of operation) in all countries except Uruguay where no special ruling exists.

Warrant Deposit. This is required by both national and foreign companies in Bolivia, Brazil, Colombia, Spain, Mexico, Portugal, Uruguay, and Venezuela. It is required only by foreign companies in Argentina and Chile. It is not required at all in Ecuador, Paraguay, and Peru.

Authorization to Operate in Direct Insurance. This is mandatory if legal prerequisites are met in Argentina, Bolivia, Chile, Ecuador, Spain, Mexico, Paraguay, Peru, Portugal, Uruguay, and Venezuela. It is discretional in Brazil and Colombia. When authorization is denied, recourse exists in Argentina (executive authority), Brazil (president of the republic), Colombia (replacement), Ecuador (Supreme Court), Spain (administrative law action), Paraguay (replacement and administrative law action), Peru (executive authority), and Venezuela (Ministry of Development).

Policies. Authorization is required by the responsible official organizations in all countries. Standard forms for certain branches exist in Argentina, Brazil, Colombia, Ecuador, Mexico, Portugal, and Venezuela, and for all forms of insurance in Peru and Uruguay.

Rates. Authorization of the responsible official organizations is required

142

in all countries. Uniform rates for certain branches exist in Brazil, Columbia, Spain, Mexico, and Portugal, and in all branches in Chile, Paraguay, and Uruguay.

Private Insurances Which Are Compulsory. Argentina—insurance for spectators at sports events.

Bolivia—fire insurance for creditors.

Brazil—third party vehicle insurance, export credit insurance, company property fire and transport insurance, personal injury to civil aviation insurance, transporters third party insurance, and real estate fire insurance on cooperative apartment houses.

Colombia—fidelity and performance bond insurance, transporters third party insurance, and third party vehicle insurance.

Chile—accident insurance for municipal transport passengers.

Ecuador—third party vehicle insurance.

Spain—third party vehicle insurance, hunting insurance, and travel insurance.

Mexico—travel insurance, integral agricultural and live stock insurance.

Paraguay—passenger insurance.

Peru—employee life insurance, decreasing mortgage duty life insurance.

Portugal—insurance covering employees of industry and commerce, occupational hazard insurance, and municipal transport insurance.

Uruguay—occupational illnesses and accident insurance, accident insurance for civil servants while performing their work, air insurance, and fire and damage by elevators insurance.

Authorization to Operate in Reinsurance. In all countries this is automatic for companies operating in direct insurance. There are the following stipulations: (1) in Brazil it is mandatory to accept retrocessions of the IRB even though the company does not operate in direct insurance, (2) in Chile a company is prohibited from operating only in reinsurance, (3) in Venezuela prerequisites of capital stock minimums and warrant deposits must be met.

Special Limitations on Reinsurance Activity. In Argentina company must cede to INDER the surplus of net retentions. In Brazil the surplus must be placed in the IRB that retrocedes in Brazil or in foreign markets. In Colombia a company must cede the part of the risks that exceed 20% of capital stock and reserves. In Chile surpluses not placed in the national market must be passed to the Reinsurance Bank. In Ecuador all reinsurance contracts must be approved by the Supervisory Office. Ceding and accepting between parent companies and their affiliates is prohibited in Mexico. In Peru the National Bank has the exclusive right to all reinsurance operations in and of foreign countries.

Insurance Agents. Official authorization is required before a person can serve as intermediary in all countries except Argentina, Peru, and Portugal.

Control Organizations. The following serve as control organizations:

Argentina—Insurance Supervisory Office; Bolivia—Control Division of the Bank Supervisory Office; Brazil—National Committee on Private Insurance and, as a delegated organization, the Private Insurance Supervisory Office; Colombia—Banking Supervisory Office and the National Supervisory Office of Cooperative Associations; Chile—Insurance Company Supervisory Office (Board of Insurance Directors); Spain—Assistant Board of Directors of Insurance; Mexico—National Secretary of the Treasury and Public Credit and the National Banking Commission on Insurance and Sureties; Paraguay—Bank Supervisory Office; Peru—Supervisory Office of Banks and Insurance; Portugal—Insurance Inspectorate; Uruguay—General Inspectorate of the Treasury and Stock Companies; Venezuela—Insurance Supervisory Office.

Official Bodies that Operate in the Private Insurance Market. These include the following: Argentina—National Postal Savings Bank, National Aeronautical Insurance Company, and INDER (reinsurance); Brazil—IRB (in reinsurance operations); Colombia—Territorial Credit Institute; Agricultural, Industrial, and Mining Credit Bank; La Previsora S.A.; National Provision Fund; Colombian Institute of Social Security and the Exportation Promotion Fund; Chile—Reinsurance Bank, National Institute of Insurances of the State, National Credit for Exportation Insurance Company, and the State Bank of Chile; Spain—Insurance Compensation Consortium, Comissary of Obligatory Travel Insurance, National Guarantee Fund for Traffic Risks, and the Sociedad de Seguro de Crédito a la Exportación, S.A.; Mexico—Aseguradora Mexicana S.A., Aseguradora Nacional Agrícola y Ganadera S.A., Aseguradora Hidalgo S.A., and Compañía Mexicana de Seguro de Crédito, S.A.; Peru—National Bank (reinsurance); Portugal—Credit Insurance Company; Uruguay—Insurance Bank of the State.

Appendix II

LEGISLATION AND SUPERVISION OF INSURANCE
IN DEVELOPING COUNTRIES

Because of the extraordinary interest in insurance activities in developing countries, we reproduce below the report which was drafted by a group of experts at the request of the United National Conference on Trade and Development (UNCTAD) and was presented to the Secretary General of this conference.

This group, which conducted its duties in Geneva from 19–20 July, 1971, was composed of the following individuals: Sra. Gregoria C. Arnaldo, (Manilla, Philippines) Insurance Commissioner, president of the Asiatic Association of Insurance Directors; Mr. Sadettin Barlas (Istanbul, Turkey), president of the Supervision Council of Insurance in Turkey; Sr. Giuseppe Corso (Rome, Italy), general inspector of the Supervision Service of Insurance in Italy, president of the work group Financial Guarantees of the Insurance Commission of the OCDE; M. Saad Kanouni (Rabat, Morroco), finance inspector and assistant manager of the Insurance Service of Morroco; Mr. Abdurrahaman M. Khalfe (Karachi, Pakistan), insurance commissioner, head of Insurance Department; Mr. Samuel O. Keku (Lagos, Nigeria), insurance superintendent, federal minister of Trade (Insurance Division); Mr. Moustafa Rajab (Baghdad, Iraq), Iraqui Insurance Company, former insurance commissioner; Mr. Paul Emmanuel Ramamabe (Tanarive, Madagascar), head of Insurance Service; president of the International Conference on Insurance Inspection of the African States, France and Malgache; general advisor of the Afianzadora Mexicana, Mexico, former director of the National Insurance Commission; Mr. Lars Erik Toren, vice-president of the Swedish Insurance Control Service; Sr. Augusto J. Vazquez (Buenos Aires, Argentina), insurance superintendent; Sr. Eduardo Wallis (Caracas, Venezuela), insurance superintendent, Finance Ministry. Mr. Gabriel Paratte, director of Patria, Swiss Life Insurance Company; former president of work group on insurance legislation of the OCDE Insurance Commission, served as advisor.

Introduction

1. In accordance with instructions given by the Intangible Goods Trade Commission and that of financing related to trade in its first sessions period held in December 1965 and approved by the Trade and Development Board in its third period of sessions, the UNCTAD secretariat prepared a study on the legislative systems and supervision of insurance in developing countries. In

this study analysis is made of legislation and supervision existing in developing countries regarding insurance companies. The Commission, during its second period of sessions also took note of private insurance in Europe. The necessary information for the preparation of the UNCTAD secretariat study was obtained, in accordance with the Commission's instructions, from interested governments through their answers to a questionnaire on legislation and supervision of insurance and reinsurance markets. The questionnaire was prepared by the secretary with the aid of advisors who were familiar with similar problems brought up in the preparation of the OCDE study. The questionnaire was distributed to interested governments at the beginning of 1967.

2. During its second group of sessions the Commission asked the Secretary General of UNCTAD to "in due time, convene a meeting of insurance supervisors and other experts from developing countries to make an analysis and formulate observations on the studies of the secretariat based on answers to the questionnaire with respect to legislation, supervision, and insurance market."

3. The meeting of the group of experts was convened by the Secretary General of UNCTAD in Geneva 19–30 July 1971.

4. The group expressed satisfaction for the study prepared by the secretariat on the insurance legislation and appreciation for the complete detailed information set forth on the different legislative systems and insurance supervision in developing countries. The experts agreed that the subjects dealt with in the ten chapters of the descriptive study could serve as a basis for the different insurance supervision elements in the same order as they appeared in the study. Some participants thought that special attention should be given in the debate to various subjects since the secretariat's study did not clarify them enough. Nevertheless, the general opinion was that the study, just as it was, was adapted to the objectives it had been prepared for and it was not necessary to revise it. Determined questions that the participants wished to analyze in greater detail or outline in a special way could be submitted to discussion when the corresponding study chapter was being examined.

5. Apart from the study, the experts had two other UNCTAD documents for their information: the report on international level institution of a unified statistics system for insurance and the report on technical reserves investment in the country where premium income is received.

Finalities and Objectives of Insurance Supervision

1. There was general agreement that insurance supervision is a necessity for the adequate development of insurance activities, and these activities if adequately supervised play an outstanding role in the economic growth process of all countries. The participants expressed the opinion that legislation on insurance activities should always offer the basis for continuous

supervision of insurance companies with the object of guaranteeing fulfillment of legislation in all aspects. They also pointed out that insurance supervision, without endangering the traditional function for which it is intended—protection of insurees, beneficiaries, and third parties—should also constantly bear in mind economic and social interests and other national interests. For example the importance was underlined in insurance supervision for coordinating insurance company investments with the economic policy of the state. They discussed the necessity of impeding the outflow of foreign currency which could cause excessive utilization of foreign insurance and reinsurance company services. In the opinion of the experts another important task of insurance supervision in developing countries is the establishment and reinforcement of the national insurance market since a solid national market is essential for economic development. Diverse legislative measures could be adopted to obtain this objective since they would protect national insurance companies, enabling them to develop and absorb an important part of the national insurance market. The participants thought that the question of whether national insurance companies should be public, private or semipublic should be weighed with the economic and social system of each country with the goal that each have a solid efficient national insurance market providing efficient service to the national community. The experts also underlined the usefulness of ethical commercial competition.

2. Regarding the state supervisory system which insurance legislation should institute, the participants unanimously thought that a purely formal supervision would not only be inadequate but could be damaging for the interests concerned since it could create an erroneous public impression on the extent of supervision. Supervision of the financial status of insurance companies would be inadequate too since other aspects such as rates and fair treatment of the insuree are also considered essential elements for the protection of the public. Thus the experts were inclined to extend supervision to all activities of insurance companies, especially aspects giving rise to excessive profits, or abusive or prejudicial practices for the insuree. Consequently the imposition of efficient control on activities of insurance companies was strongly upheld. Some participants thought this control should not slow down the ordinary activities of insurance companies since it could paralyze their commercial initiative and transactions. Supervisory personnel should have adequate discretional intervention powers to exercise good judgment and adopt prompt and efficient measures when the situation justified their doing so.

3. The participants discussed whether different types of supervisory systems should be applied according to type of insurance transactions. Although the participants agreed that all transactions should be subject to supervision since all have a direct relation with the financial solidity of the insurance companies, they felt emphasis should be placed on supervising transactions

involving necessities of insurees—those with social aspects, those which entail long-term commitments, and those where the beneficiary and subscriber of the policy are not the same person. Life insurance, small property insurance, and civil responsibility insurance are important examples of transactions requiring special supervision. The participants feel that special measures regulating rates and policy conditions should be adopted for compulsory insurances.

4. The question of prohibiting insurance of national risks abroad was exhaustively discussed. The experts accept the principle that to encourage the establishment and expansion of a national insurance market in developing countries national risks (risks relative to goods located in the country and to residents of the country) as well as responsibility for these risks should be insured only by national and foreign companies established in the country and authorized by national authorities. The contracting of insurance abroad should be accepted only when the risk cannot be covered in the country. In this event authorization is required from supervisory groups provided that these transactions are registered and controlled adequately. In addition, the authorities should adopt as many measures as possible for helping the national market with the object of increasing the number and types of national risks covered in the country itself, thus reducing the necessity of obtaining special coverage abroad. In this respect, reinsurance could carry out a useful function in proper cases.

5. The experts do not consider it a good idea to establish an exception to the above in the case of important international companies, which apply for permission to insure all risks incurred in many countries, through a single worldwide coverage from their headquarters.

6. Discussing mandatory insurance, the experts underlined the importance that most insurance forms for damages to third parties (automobile, agricultural, etc.) should be compulsory. Likewise they examined the question of limiting compulsory third party damage insurance to injury or extending it to material damages as well. Although they felt the latter was preferable, the first could be applied as an initial measure for maintaining the value of premiums within the reach of the insured public. The participants are particularly interested in quick payment,and premium cost, especially in the case of automotive insurance. Supervisory authorities should have the right to intervene to guarantee fairness of premiums and policy conditions. Especially they should prevent excessive insurance costs, primarily through commission control on policy contracting, which should be suppressed or reduced to the minimum. Premiums covering risks should be maintained at a proper level in relation to the costs of disasters.

7. They examined the possibility of establishing other compulsory insurances such as fire, harvest, etc., as well as risks of natural disasters such as hurricanes, avalanches, earthquakes, etc. The experts were unable to come up

with a recommendation for universal application, so they decided that developing countries should examine each case separately according to their own circumstances.

Previous Authorization for Undertaking Insurance Operations

1. All experts agreed on the necessity of requiring authorization for insurance companies and insisted that formal recording in a register is not enough. This needs to be preceded by a detailed examination of the company's economic and technical conditions, plan of operations for the future, technical competence and honesty of their personnel, dispositions on reinsurance, etc. They emphasized that only a conscientious analysis by supervisory authorities could provide valid conclusions and that authorities must have the right to investigate these factors since in this way dishonorable, fictitious, and dummy companies usually could be prevented from organizing.

2. Some experts stated that not only companies but insurance brokers as well need authorization. They particularly referred to brokers who worked for foreign companies not established in the country who issue policies abroad. The experts unanimously recommend stringent control on activities of such brokers who should be prohibited from issuing policies abroad without authorization and who should register and state which type of operations are to be conducted.

3. When granting authorization to branches or agencies of foreign companies the experts agree that criteria (technical, economic, etc.) should be similar to that applied to national companies; the technical competence and morals of foreign companies, branch directors and agents should be examined carefully. Authorization should be granted to companies, especially foreign companies, according to norms applied in the country and in relation to the needs of the national insurance market.

4. Authorization should be conceded for the principal activity branches. Life insurance and other types should have different authorizations. Some countries did not grant authorization to the same company for life insurance and other types. It was recommended to subdivide other types of insurance (accident, fire, automobile, maritime, credit, etc.) However, these subdivisions should not be excessive since this would complicate issuing policies for adequate coverage of various risks.

5. Opinions were unfavorable on limiting authorization duration. Insurance laws should give the supervisory authorities the power to cancel authorizations when the technical, economic or legal status of a company indicates.

6. In regard to limitations on business volume a company should be given authorization only when a competent entity can guarantee reaching a minimum business figure, and this limitation would be indicated only when insurance market concentration was necessary. Yet, such a stipulation needs to be made since under other conditions grave difficulties could emerge.

Legal Conditions for Realization of Insurance Operations

1. The experts agreed that both stock companies and mutuals should be considered appropriate legal forms for insurance companies as both classes could offer a guarantee of permanency, a requisite which is important in insurance due to its long-term nature. Individuals could not be insurers as they cannot offer this guarantee.

2. Each form presents advantages and disasvantages. Stock companies have an adequate means of reuniting capital and relatively easy administration; thus, they constitute a flexible element in the insurance market. However, sometimes they tend to place profit motives ahead of other considerations to the detriment of the insuree's interests, especially in profit sharing with insurees. A stock company can fall into the hands of reduced groups, e.g., families, and lose their true anonymous character. Therefore the experts recommend that only nominative shares be authorized so that officials should know at all times to whom a given company belongs.

3. Mutual companies usually don't have commercial goals but are constituted to satisfy stated interests of their members. For many branches of insurance mutual companies could recommended where similar but unimportant risks must be covered with a determined group of persons (either a large or small group). In more complex companies, mutual companies tend to have a behavior similar to that of stock companies if they have to resort to the market to sell policies to the public; in this event they act as stock companies with no shareholders. True mutuals represent an adequate solution from the negotiation point of view. In some countries the organization of mutuals is encouraged in the life branch, providing they exceed a certain size.

4. The experts have established a distinction between national companies, foreign company affiliates, and foreign company branches and agencies. While the nationality of the first and last did not bring up any special problem, sometimes it was difficult to determine the nationality of the affiliates, especially when foreign-owned companies did not present themselves as such but appeared to be true national companies. The experts agreed that to qualify as a national company, it has to be constituted according to the country's laws and that its headquarters must be in the country in question. Some experts felt that the nationality of the shareholders was another criteria. They emphasized that for a company to be considered national the majority of the corporate capital had to be in the hands of country nationals.

5. The experts agreed that insurance companies must work only in the branches and dedicate themselves only to operations directly related to insurance. Supervisory officials must stop them from working in any mercantile activity other than insurance.

6. They also agreed on the necessity of promulgating a law regulating insurance contract content. In compulsory insurance contracts must be uniform. In other types of insurance dispositions regulating the most important

policy conditions must be fulfilled as well, and the authorities must control policies so as not to permit detrimental, obscure, or ambiguous conditions for policy takers. However, companies should have enough liberty and resouurces to experiment with and improve policy types offered so that policy takers could understand their rights and obligations better. However, legal precision should not be lost in the process.

7. They also examined reinsurance contracts. The experts agreed that the legal form and conditions of these contracts did not exact the precise control recommended for policy models and conditions of direct contracts since it was assumed that the integrating parties possessed the same technical and professional level. However, the group recommended that reinsurance contracts be submitted regularly to the supervisory authorities, at least for their information, so that they could intervene when contractual conditions were clearly contrary to law. By controlling reinsurance contracts the authorities could prove such problems as fronting operations (coverage by concealed foreign interests), an excessive proportion of operations abroad, insufficient reinsurance, inadequate commission collection, etc. In addition, authorities should not try to direct the companies by mixing too much in their reinsurance plans.

8. Supervisors must be trained until they can give decisions on reinsurance matters and help companies find the best solution. The group recommended that UNCTAD participate in creating training courses of this type.

9. The participants also discussed portfolio transfers from one company to another and thought it necessary that authorities in countries where this operated efficiently should be in charge of regulating these transfers. Naturally their decisions must be based on interests of insurees of both companies making the transfer as well as of the company receiving them. Consent of the individual policy holder does not appear necessary, but he should have the privilege of rescinding the contract if he wishes.

10. The question of privileged credits for insurees and third party beneficiaries was discussed. It was agreed that there should be special privileges on property destined for coverage of technical reserves of some insurance branches (for example, life) and a general privilege on all property of the insurance company.

Financial Conditions Relative to Funds Belonging to Insurance Companies

1. Regarding initial corporative capital, the experts recommend that minimum quantities be fixed according to conditions in each country and according to class and volume of business forecast by the company applying for authorization. In addition to the initial capital, a supplementary organization fund had to be exacted to cover costs of establishment and initial company operations. Although the initial corporative capital should be saved entirely once the company got underway (possibly readjusted in depreciation cases),

this supplementary contribution for the organization period of the company could be used up.

2. After the company is off to a good start the experts said that it would be good to accumulate free reserves for gradually assuming a predominant role, comparable to that enacted by corporate capital in the initial phase. Some stressed that excess corporative capital could even be detrimental for insurees since this should be producing profits. Nevertheless, it would be necessary to resort to subscription of new capital in shares if the increased free reserves were not enough to provide a margin of solvency (corporative capital plus free reserves) similar to the type and volume of operation undertaken by the company.

3. The experts pointed out that different names are given to free reserves in different countries but that no matter what the name, these reserves are most important since they improve the insured portfolio guarantee, creating a safeguard against adverse fluctuations. Thus they increase the retention power of the company and strengthen both the company and the national market. Therefore part of the annual profits could be dedicated to forming these free reserves. They also considered essential the maintenance of a solvency margin where company credit exceeds obligations by a minimum sum fixed according to transaction volume and portfolio composition.

Financial Conditions Relative to Insurance Company Technical Reserves

1. The experts agreed unanimously that technical reserves constitute the most important item of insurance company liabilities and that they are essential and should be evaluated precisely and rigorously scrutinized and censored. They studied the three principal types of technical reserves: mathematical, current risks, and pending disaster reserves.

2. The group considered that satisfactory methods exist and are usually applied universally for evaluating life insurance reserves containing a savings element and those for covering pure risk life policies.

3. The experts accepted the principal that current reserve risks, as well as all other types of reserves, had to consider future obligations of the insurance company. Therefore they should be calculated in a prospective manner, based on experience and remembering observed tendencies; they should cover obligations and future costs throughout the risk period and should not be connected to premiums, especially when there is no assurrance that rates are adequate. Some countries already base current risks reserves evaluation on this principle.

4. They also examined methods for calculating current risks reserves, including the "block" evaluation to the "policy by policy prorated" evaluation. The experts considered separate evaluations to be essential for each insurance branch. They also recommended frequent verification of block rating validity, keeping losses in mind and distribution of premiums throughout the year.

5. Pending disaster reserves supervision often presented serious difficulties, especially the auditing of reserves calculated in accordance with the "case-by-case" method when the company had a large volume of transactions. However, in some of these chaotic situations, especially in branches with a large volume (automobiles, etc.), a procedure based on statistical extrapolation was possible and considered preferable. This involved projection in a given year of all adjustments of the average costs and frequency of losses recorded in the past. At any rate, it was recommended that a company carry out *a posteriori* verification of evaluations of preceding fiscal years.

6. On the question of technical reserves for risks ceded in reinsurance, the experts unanimously recommended the constitution of gross reserves by the ceding company, both for current risks and pending losses. They agreed on the possibility of considering, at least partially, credits over reinsurers as acceptable assets for covering these reserves. Nevertheless, it was proved that in cases where these credits could be partially accepted for covering technical reserves, the reinsurers should designate the corresponding assets toward covering these reserves.

Investment, Location and Deposit of Insurance Company Funds

1. The group concurred with the recommendation of the Conference on Trade and Development that funds should be invested principally in the country where premiums originate. They indicated that the document they had received from the UNCTAD secretary proposed measures to the Intangible Goods Trade Commission and that of financing related to trade by which developing countries could put this recommendation into practice. Within the limitations of such a recommendation, the experts agreed that in the investment of insurance company property they had to remember the three requisites of safety, profitability, and liquidity. Moreover, the property portfolio of each company must be sufficiently diversified. Such a portfolio should not accept speculative type investments. Although it is paramount to act with caution in investing shares, this does not mean that some good blue chip stock market shares are not suitable. To safeguard the principle that insurance companies not involve themselves in business outside of insurance, the company holding shares or securities belonging to another company should be maintained at a minimum to avoid all possibility that a dominant participation be acquired.

2. The group examined methods of publishing lists of authorized investments and decided that due to important differences in capital markets of various countries, it was impossible to prepare these lists on an international basis—it must be done country by country. Foreign values usually should not be accepted; however, exceptions might arise in individual cases, and these could be authorized by competent authorities for each case. They recommended that the monetary concurrence principle be respected and that commitments in a currency determined by assets in that currency are cov-

ered. The group further recommended that each country be flexible in indicating authorized investments which still would have to measure up to two objectives—safety of the company and protection of interests of the nation.

3. The experts recommended that each country use the most appropriate method, considering local conditions, of evaluating assets in the balance of each insurance company. Nevertheless, evaluation should be made using prudent and conservative criteria so that sufficient coverage was truly provided for the asset. While obligation evaluation, especially when quoted on the stock exchange, do not present difficulty, shares securities suffer sudden sharp fluctuations. Some experts recommended that a special reserve for proportional leveling be created to counteract value fluctuations of these securities. The purchase price or real estate is an adequate basis for its evaluation unless dealing with properties purchased a long time ago where value had increased considerably. Then reevaluation was recommended to give policy owners participation in the capital earnings from purchases they had contributed to in the financing. If this reevaluation was unjustifiably postponed, profits from these capital earnings would benefit policy owners who had not originally financed the purchases.

4. Assets to cover technical reserves, despite the type of business and for both national and foreign companies, should be located in the country where premiums originated. The group agreed that reserves constituting a direct complement of technical reserves—such as prescribed leveling, fluctuation, etc.—should maintain local norms for technical reserves. They unanimously agreed that reserves for profit distribution among policy holders (earning surplus) should be kept in common with mathematical reserves. Some recommended cooperation between insurance supervision authorities of the receiving and originating company regarding nonlocalized corporative capital and free reserves of foreign companies. This was needed to verify their existence in other countries, especially in the company headquarters countries. This cooperation would provide an exact evaluation of the global solvency of a determined insurance company.

5. The actual presence in the country of the asset elements for coverage of technical reserves and their complements is not an easy way to verify the location of the assets. A convenient way would be to exact all assets to be deposited in a state bank or public entity. Even this method would have drawbacks since for an essentially financial company such as an insurance company freezing assets could be detremental to its useful administration. Whenever the deposit method is applied to technical reserve deposits, companies should be given facilities to permit rational negotiations—to provide an easy substitution of those assets if the company decided to do so and has approval of supervisory authorities. Deposits should be made in a trustworthy institution unrelated financially to any insurance company, and preferably a public institution.

6. Many experts thought that supervisory authorities should have power to order a general freeze of all insurance company assets not already deposited, providing they had reason to believe the company was facing difficulties regarding paying its debts. This way authorities could keep a company from freely liquidating assets before providing protection for insurees and third-party beneficiaries.

Technical, Commercial and Accounting Negotiations of Insurance Companies

1. The group agreed unanimously that rates, costs, reinsurance contracts, accounting, and statistics are the primary negotiation elements of insurance companies.

2. They also agreed that authorities should have the right to approve or reject rates for life insurance and compulsory insurance other than life before their application by insurance companies. For life technical bases should be sufficient prior to approval by supervisory authorities. The group discussed the establishment of uniform rates by authorities, insurance associations, etc., and decided that the entity responsible for establishing rates was unimportant since it had to be approved by the authorities.

3. Although the experts agreed that supervision could be less rigid in branches other than life and facultative insurance, they still favor approval of these rates as well providing this is technically possible. At least they should be presented to authorities for information and *a posteriori* control. The experts recommended the use of rate establishing organs for rates of insurance other than life.

4. The experts agreed that authorities should control tariffs and prohibit both insufficient and excessively high rates to protect the interests of policy owners. Not only should rates provide company solvency, but they should also reflect the costs and aptness of services furnished.

5. The group agreed that income from investments covering technical reserves should be kept in mind when calculating rates (reducing them) or should be given the policy holders (profit participation).

6. All current costs of insurance companies, particularly paid commissions, should be controlled constantly. Acquisition commissions paid to agents and intermediaries should be in proportion to services offered the public. The commission in compulsory insurance must be small as was stated in Chapter 1. Some experts recommended that different maximum commission rates be set in the various compulsory insurance branches. All agreed that no discount should be conceded to policy holders. Dividend distribution among shareholders should not be carried out without previous revision of authorities.

7. The experts reemphasized the importance of reinsurance contracts, particularly regarding business volume retained by the company. Authorities must be informed of these contracts and must furnish advice here but without trying to direct the company by mixing too much in the insurance

plan drafting. Some maintained that if national reinsurance regulation was too flexible, reinsurance conditions should be made more difficult for companies. Others felt that co-insurance and national pools could sometimes help obtain adequate national coverage regarding risks exceeding retention capacity of one company and still increase the volume of business retained on the national market.

8. The group stressed that annual reports to supervisory authorities (including balances, profits and losses, and other states) was one of the most important instruments for efficient insurance supervision. Although the UNCTAD secretary, with help from another group of experts, prepared a study concerned with insurance statistics problems which was presented to the Commissions of Intangible Goods Trade and Financing Related to Trade, the group preferred to abstain from proposing any detailed statistical system. They recommended nevertheless that developing countries should adopt an adequate analytical statistics system to be used both by national and foreign companies established in the country. Their object should be extended use of such a system (divided by branches, etc.) and its normalization; they supported efforts by UNCTAD in trying to attain these objectives through proposal of an international unified insurance statistics system.

9. The experts praised the advantages of specialization and insisted that even in cases where the same company operated in life and in other branches, the administration of each of these two types should be separate, including accounting, investment, etc. This separation should be reflected in the annual report presented to supervisors.

Regime Applicable to Active Reinsurance Operations (Acceptances)

1. The group established a distinction between national and foreign companies regarding reinsurance acceptances (active reinsurance). They unanimously agreed that some control was needed over accepted business but that this control should be different from supervision over direct operations and should be limited to recording data and not to material vigilance. Reinsurance operations by national companies operating in direct insurance should be supervised more closely since a risky reinsurance acceptance policy could compromise the stability of the company and endanger its direct insurance portfolio. They agreed that supervision of national professional reinsurance companies should be general and that authorities should abstain from going into detail and assuming responsibility in the guarantee of operations and general negotiations of the reinsurance company.

2. Some referred to the possible favorable effects on some incipient insurance markets from the existence of a national reinsurance company totally or partially belonging to the state, obligating all companies to cede a percentage of each risk subscribed in the country. Advantages of such an institution are guaranteed registration of all transactions in the country,

including rates and technical results; adequate increase of retention capacity of the national market; redistribution of risks among national companies; increase of negotiation power compared to international reinsurance market through common accessibility to a mass of premiums. Although the group recognized the usefulness of such institutions, some felt that the required cession system should be temporary. They also agreed that required cession rates should not be too high since this would slow down development of national ceding companies instead of promoting them.

3. They agreed that it was not necessary to establish foreign reinsurance companies in the country to be able to accept reinsurance operations with them. They estimated that supervision of these operations should take place through national ceding companies by proper supervision of their reinsurance cessions. They felt that taxes on reinsurance premiums of accepted operations were technically objectionable and should be avoided.

4. They also examined investments of accepted reinsurance business technical reserves and agreed that a solution had to be found in each case according to which the ceding company was or was not obligated to keep the assets in its position. In cases where the ceding company constituted gross technical reserves and equally constituted assets corresponding to the coverage, the reinsurer must abstain from repeating the same coverage; the credits on the direct insurer should be considered in this case as acceptable assets for coverage of corresponding reinsurance reserves.

Organization of Insurance Supervision Services

1. The group agreed that due to the specific and technical nature of their functions, insurance supervisors should constitute an independent, high-level branch of public administration, directly responsible to a high-level official. This was justified by the fact that supervisory authority, within the framework of insurance legislation, exercises its control in the complementary and technical fields of insurance, having ample intervention powers. Technical or economic decisions of the supervisory authority must not be annulled by other departments. Nevertheless, activities of the supervisory authority should be controlled by a superior, such as the government, judicial power, etc.

2. Such responsibility required that insurance inspection personnel have first-class technical qualifications. The control organ director or its board members plus high officials must be highly competent, particularly in judicial, economic, accounting, and acturial matters. Continuity is needed in insurance supervision functions.

3. Some experts, recognizing the usefulness of intervention of supervisors in the solution of litigation between companies and insurees, declared that supervisors should abstain from intervening in justice court competence. Other experts indicated the advantage of policy holders being able to resolve

small differences in a more friendly fashion, entrusting this task to the supervisory authority. All experts supported official intervention by an authority to speed up direct negotiations between parties in a litigation on insurance questions.

4. The group unanimously felt that publication of a complete annual report (national monograph) by the supervisory authority would be an extremely important function since this would furnish useful data on the insurance market. They recommended the interchange of these annual reports among supervisory authorities in different countries, especially when accompanied by a translated summary. They agreed that uniformity of the statistics in the report would considerably improve the understanding and usage of the reports.

5. The group voted for cooperation among insurance commissioners of various countries for interchanging experience and data. The UNCTAD secretary promised to help establish such contacts among commissioners.

6. The group felt it would be useful to create a permanent advisory organ of representatives of different professional groups and other groups interested in insurance to make suggestions to the supervisory authority on problems relative to the insurance market due to the complexity of insurance operations and the role of insurance in the economy. Definitive decisions, however, should be left to the supervisory authority.

7. Whether or not the above group was created, the experts felt that determined tasks could be assigned to certain institutions, such as professional organizations, which could provide useful functions for insurance supervision under the control of the authorities. For example, authorization of agents by authorities could remain subject to prerequisites determined by insurer or agents associations based on minimum conditions of technical capacity and trustworthiness of candidates.

8. Although supervisors should be adequately trained to fulfill the complex tasks within their range, the group indicated that developing countries often find it difficult to undertake such training on a national level, especially for high officials. They examined the possibility of organizing this training on a regional or interregional basis, and the participation of UNCTAD was recommended in this program. The group stressed the importance of careful selection of candidates who should already know the insurance material. Courses also should be oriented toward problems and questions of insurance supervision.

Nationalization of the Insurance Industry

1. The group repeated the opinion that the question of whether insurance bodies should be public, private, or semipublic was a matter to be decided by each country according to their economic and social system. The essential factor was that every country should have a solid and efficient national

insurance market to provide adequate coverage at reasonable rates. The group reviewed a study by the secretary and heard explanations of an expert from a country which had nationalized the insurance and reinsurance industry.

2. The interesting information provided by this expert covered many technical aspects of nationalization such as structure of the nationalized market, negotiation problems, investments, and promotion. He stressed that the nationalized insurance industry has no difficulties in functioning on a firm technical basis. The group decided that nationalization, although it created a new form of market, did not essentially change the nature of technical problems which an insurance market, private or nationalized, must solve to function properly. The group was pleased to note that recommendations formulated in this report were usually valid in the particular case of a nationalized market.